The Seniors Guide to
PC Basics

Notices

The Seniors Guide to PC Basics

is published by
Gateway, Inc.
14303 Gateway Place
Poway, CA 92064

Version 1.0

ISBN: 1-57729-299-5

DATE: 10-16-03

Printed in the United States of America

Distributed in the United States by Gateway, Inc.

Welcome

From the overview of personal computers in Chapter 1 through a look at tips and troubleshooting in Chapter 11, *The Seniors Guide to PC Basics* provides you with what you need to know to use your PC to its fullest potential. This product is designed to accommodate your learning style, and to make learning easy, interesting, and fun. You can stick to just the bare essentials or learn in greater depth by practicing key skills and applying your new knowledge. Our goal is to show you how technology can enhance your life, provide some fun, and open up new opportunities.

Classroom Learning

A hands-on training course on this subject is offered to enhance and improve your skills. Classes are held at Gateway® stores nationwide and additional fees may apply. Our classes are ideal solutions for people who want to become knowledgeable and get up and running in just three hours. They provide the opportunity to learn from one of our experienced and friendly instructors and practice important skills with other students. Call 888-852-4821 for enrollment information. One of our representatives will assist you in selecting a time and location that is convenient for you. If applicable, please have your Gateway customer ID and order number ready when you call. Please refer to your Gateway paperwork for this information.

More Than a Book

The Seniors Guide to PC Basics is more than a book; it is a blended learning system that also includes a CD-ROM and Internet presentations and activities. These tools all work together to provide a truly unique learning experience. The book presents technical information in visual, practical, and understandable ways. The CD-ROM extends the book by providing additional material on the subject. Continue learning online by logging on to www.LearnwithGateway.com. The enrollment key provided with this book gives you access to additional content and interactive exercises. This Web site allows us to keep you updated on rapidly changing information and new software releases.

Contents

Contents

Contents

How to Use This Book

As you read the chapters in this book, you'll find pictures, figures, and diagrams to help reinforce key ideas and concepts. You'll also find pictures or icons that serve as cues to flag important information or provide directions. Here is a guide to help you understand the icons you'll encounter in this book:

 A Note identifies a relatively important piece of information that will make things easier or faster for you to accomplish on your PC. Most notes are worth reading, if only for the time and effort they can save you.

 A Warning gives notice that an action on your PC can have serious consequences and could lead to loss of work, delays, or other problems. Our goal is not to scare you, but to steer you clear of potential sources of trouble.

You'll find sidebar information spread throughout the chapters, as follows:

> ### More About . . .
>
> The More About . . . information is supplementary, and is provided so you can learn more about making technology work for you. Feel free to skip this material during your first pass through the book, but please return to it later.

You can use each part of our innovative Survive & Thrive™ learning system by itself, or combine them for the ultimate learning experience.

 Come to a class at your local Gateway® store and enjoy a face-to-face learning experience with one of our expert instructors. Our state-of-the-art facilities and interactive approach are designed to build your new skills quickly – and let you have fun at the same time.

 Learn at your own pace using the enclosed full-color book. It combines high-tech images and concise overviews with simple instructions to create an ideal guide and ongoing reference.

 Enter the exciting world of online learning at www.LearnwithGateway.com, the Web site that delivers high-quality instruction the way you want it, when you want it.

 Immerse yourself in the enclosed CD bonus materials. Simply insert the CD into your PC, and go. That's all it takes to launch the innovative extras we've included.

Join the Computer Age!

Times change and people change with them. Almost everywhere you look today, someone is using a personal computer. A personal computer (often called a PC) is a machine that, put simply, gathers and processes information and then presents it back to you. You can use a PC to type letters, keep track of items, listen to music, play games, perform calculations, and interact with other people.

When you first look at a computer, because of all the equipment and cables involved, it can appear quite intimidating and mystifying. In this book, you will discover how to use your computer with ease and confidence and dispel much of the mystery surrounding it. This chapter explains how computers evolved and some of the many uses of computers. You will also learn about the different elements of a computer such as a tower, processor, memory and storage devices, and how each of them play an important role in helping you accomplish your computer goals.

Exploring the History of Personal Computers

A PC (see Figure 1-1) is just one type of computer. In fact, computers come in all shapes and sizes. A computer can be so large that it fills a room, or so small it could get lost in a desk drawer. Computers are all around you, even though they're not always obvious—they're built into automated teller machines (ATMs), microwave ovens, children's toys, and even the digital radio in your car.

Although you can purchase a PC from a local store, over the phone, or online almost as easily as making airline reservations, you might not realize how much technology and history are behind the PC you use today.

Figure 1-1 A typical modern personal computer.

In its most basic form, a computer is a device that manipulates numbers, or computes. The earliest known computing device was an abacus, as shown in Figure 1-2. Although the abacus is not an actual "computer," it made complex arithmetic easier to understand and apply.

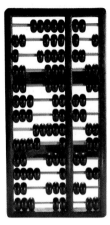

In 1642, Blaise Pascal took computing devices to the next level when he invented a numerical wheel calculator. Once mechanical devices provided a means to manipulate numbers, the rush to make the best "computer" was on! Early computers were basically calculators, used mainly to handle arithmetic. The least expensive calculator you can find today is far more powerful and much smaller than any of these early computers (see Figure 1-3).

Figure 1-2 An abacus was one of the original computing devices.

Figure 1-3 Early models of common computer components. (US Army Photos. Courtesy of Michael John Muus.)

By the early to mid-1900s, computers were evolving from mechanical to mostly electronic in nature and were used primarily in solving mathematical problems and processing financial data. By the 1970s, most of the common components of modern PCs were in use, such as printers, tape backups, disk storage, and memory. Over the years, such devices have become more advanced and barely resemble their original forms.

In fact, the 1970s were a big decade for computers, as their uses began to expand dramatically. Basic word processing made its debut—though the first word-processing programs allowed you to erase words and letters while typing, but could do little else. Other innovations and uses for computers included the first video games, such as PONG® (see Figure 1-4) and Breakout®, the first mouse, and the first color monitor, to name just a few.

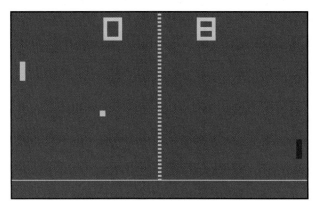

Figure 1-4 PONG for the PC (Copyright 2002 David Winter http://www.pong-story.com/).

Figure 1-5 Early-model PCs from Hewlett-Packard and Sun.

Even the Internet got its start in the 1970s. The U.S. Department of Defense, several major universities, and several research facilities developed the first network. This network linked sites in California, Utah, and Massachusetts. It enabled computers from multiple, distant locations to communicate with each other and to exchange data quickly and securely. In 1991, commercial use of the Internet began. From its humble beginnings as a pure research project, the Internet has become the fastest-growing communication medium today.

By the 1980s, computers had started to become common household items. Several companies produced PCs designed for home, office, or school use. In fact, you might recall a few of these early systems, such as Commodore®, Apple®, Texas Instruments, Tandy®, and Radio Shack (see Figure 1-5). These systems offered elementary word-processing and spreadsheet programs, basic educational software, and games.

In 1981, there were only about two million computers in use. By 1982, however, the total had jumped to more than five million. And by 1992, that number had swelled to 65 million. Today, more than 200 million computers are in use in the United States alone!

Figure 1-6 The rapid rate of expanding computer usage.

Figure 1-7 A notebook computer is small and trans-portable.

A major reason for the proliferation of computers over the past 30 years is that, thanks to advances in chip technology and miniaturization, computers have gotten faster and smaller. Some computers are so small you can carry them with you wherever you go (notebook computers), as shown in Figure 1-7. The rate at which computers develop continues to soar. In fact, computing technology has advanced more in the last five years than it did in the previous 25. If cars had developed as quickly as computers, they would fly, need refueling only every 10,000 miles, and cost only $500!

Today, computers play a part in nearly every aspect of our lives. There are many obvious uses of computers today:

- ✦ Word processing

- ✦ Communicating with e-mail, instant messaging programs, newsgroups, and chat rooms

- ✦ Surfing the Web and shopping online

- ✦ Playing music from compact discs (CDs) and MP3s, and recording music from digital instruments

- ✦ Transferring files over networks or the Internet

- ✦ Playing virtual-reality games with people across the globe

You see, a computer isn't just a box with a monitor on your desk; computers are built into many electronic devices (see Figure 1-8). Many modern conveniences couldn't exist without computers.

Figure 1-8 Computers are everywhere you look!

It's hard to predict what forms computers will take in the future. Technological advances can come at any time, and you can assume that computers will most likely continue to get faster, smaller, and cheaper.

Understanding Common PC Components

Now that you've been introduced to the modern computer, let's review some standard computer terms and basic PC components. Becoming familiar with them will help you to get the most out of this book and your PC.

Hardware and Software

The two main classifications of a PC are hardware and software. All physical objects attached to a PC (things you can touch), including the monitor, keyboard, mouse, and printer, are considered hardware. Many types of hardware devices are available for PCs; a complete list is too long to include here. We do, however, discuss many common PC devices in Chapter 2. Generally speaking, hardware devices can sometimes be called hardware, devices, or components.

Hardware is further divided into two groups by function: input and output. Input hardware is any object that is used to enter information (text, sound, or images) into a PC. Examples of input hardware include keyboards, mice, scanners, digital cameras, and microphones, as shown in Figure 1-9.

Figure 1-9 Common input devices.

Output hardware is any object that conveys something from inside the PC to the outside world. Examples of output hardware include monitors, speakers, printers, and MP3 players, as shown in Figure 1-10.

Figure 1-10 Common output devices.

Some devices are considered to be both input and output devices, including storage devices such as hard drives, floppy drives, Zip drives, and CD-RW drives. Devices that send and receive data, such as network interface cards (NICs) and modems, are input/output devices as well.

Software is a general term for "computer programs." Written in one of any number of computer languages, software tells the computer how to perform tasks. Common types of software include the following:

Operating systems. An operating system (OS) is software installed on a PC that controls the way computer hardware and software interact. In other words, an operating system creates an environment in which software can operate on a PC. Examples of Microsoft® operating systems include Windows® 98, Windows Me, Windows 2000, and Windows XP® (see Figure 1-11). Other companies produce other operating systems, such as Sun Solaris®, Apple MacOS, and Red Hat Linux®, among many others.

Figure 1-11 The standard desktop view of Windows XP, a common operating system.

Programs. The terms program, application, and software are typically used to describe the tools, utilities, or games that run on your PC. Examples of such programs include Microsoft Word (a word processor), Microsoft Excel (a spreadsheet program), WinZip® (a file-compression tool), Adobe® Acrobat® (a document viewer), Typing Tutor® (a typing trainer), and Hearts (a card game).

Device drivers. A device driver is a special type of software that allows a specific hardware object to communicate with your PC. Without a device driver, hardware devices won't work with a PC. For example, the operating system requires a print driver to tell the computer how to interact with any printer. Most hardware vendors make driver installation easy—it usually requires no more effort than inserting a CD into your PC's CD-ROM drive and clicking an icon on a pop-up menu.

System Unit

The system unit, also referred to as a case or tower, is the box that that surrounds and protects the internal components of a PC (see Figure 1-12). The primary components include:

◆ A motherboard

◆ A central processing unit (CPU)

◆ Memory cards

◆ Storage devices

◆ A power supply

Figure 1-12 A typical system unit, from the front, side, and back.

 You may encounter references to a system unit as "the CPU" (an abbreviation for central processing unit). This is technically incorrect, however, because the term CPU identifies only the main processor chip on a PC's motherboard—not the whole system unit.

Motherboard

The motherboard, sometimes called a mainboard, is the foundation of a modern PC. As shown in Figure 1-13, it features numerous sockets or ports that enable it to connect all devices in a PC, such as the CPU, memory cards, and storage devices. Each motherboard is typically designed for a specific type of CPU and memory card.

Figure 1-13 A typical motherboard.

More About . . . Motherboards

Every motherboard is different; each is designed to work with only a few specific CPUs and memory cards. Some motherboards support several types of memory, whereas most support only one type. Some motherboards can accommodate two or four CPUs, but most support only one. A motherboard that supports Intel CPUs does not support AMD CPUs, because each type of CPU uses different connectors. When you purchase a motherboard, CPU, or memory upgrade, make sure all such components are compatible.

CPU

The central processing unit (CPU) is the core component in a PC (see Figure 1-14). Sometimes referred to as the "brain" of the computer, the CPU interprets and carries

out instructions, performs all computations, and controls the devices connected to the PC. There are a variety of CPUs available on the market. A well-known company is Intel, which produces the Pentium® and Celeron® processors. Another company is AMD, which produces the Athlon and Duron processors. In most cases, CPUs from Intel or AMD can be used with Microsoft operating systems.

Figure 1-14 A CPU not connected to the motherboard.

A CPU's speed is measured in hertz. Most CPUs today run at gigahertz (GHz) speeds, while some older systems are measured in megahertz (MHz). MHz indicates how many million calculations a CPU can perform every second, while GHz indicates how many billion calculations a CPU can perform every second. Although Windows XP will run on a PC with a CPU working at a speed of 233 MHz, Microsoft recommends that your PC use a CPU that is 300 MHz or faster to achieve acceptable performance.

More About . . . CPUs

When you shop for a PC, it's important to consider the CPU speed. Most PCs on the market today include CPUs that operate at speeds of 1 GHz or faster—sometimes 2 GHz or more! Of course, the PCs with the newest, fastest CPUs tend to be more expensive than their slightly older, slightly slower predecessors. Buying one or two generations or speed levels behind whatever CPU is currently fastest can usually save you money. Besides, very few programs are designed to take full advantage of the highest speeds and advanced technologies built into the most cutting-edge CPUs. Ordinary home-user tasks such as word processing, surfing the Internet, listening to audio files, and even editing home movies rarely tax even 1 GHz CPUs.

Memory Cards

Your PC uses memory cards, also called memory sticks (see Figure 1-15), to store random access memory, more commonly called RAM. RAM temporarily stores data, software, and the operating system while the PC is operating.

Figure 1-15 A memory card.

Data is stored in RAM until you assign it a permanent file name and storage location. For example, if you type a letter in WordPad on Windows XP and then turn off the power, everything you typed will be lost. But if you save your letter to a file on a storage device before you turn off the power, you can open that file to regain access to your letter after you turn the PC back on.

RAM is a very important part of a PC; in most cases, the more RAM a PC has, the better and faster it performs, and the more tasks it can handle at the same time. So, how much RAM is enough? Windows XP Home and Professional both require at least 64 MB, but Microsoft recommends 128 MB or more. In our experience, 256 MB is usually plenty for most activities in which a home user will engage.

> **More About ... RAM**
>
> You can add RAM to a PC by inserting memory cards into the motherboard. There are many memory types and numerous memory features available. The user manual for your motherboard should indicate clearly what type of RAM it supports. In that user manual you may see some of the following names for memory components: SIMM, DIMM, SDRAM, DDR, and RDRAM. Other memory features listed in a user manual may include error checking (ECC), parity or non-parity, PC100, PC133, PC800, and PC2100. The specifics of what each of these acronyms and feature names mean are very technical. In most cases, you need to know only the type and features your PC requires.

Storage Devices

When you enter information into your PC, you will probably want to store it for future reference; that's where storage devices come in. There are several types of storage devices available for PC. The most common storage devices used today include:

- ✦ Hard drive
- ✦ CD drive
- ✦ DVD drive
- ✦ Flash drive

CD and DVD drives as well as the newer Flash drives are all examples of removable storage. That is, each uses media that can be removed from the drive itself. (The term "media" refers to the individual items such as a compact disc, DVD, memory stick, and so on that you can insert into or remove from a removable storage device.) Other older types of removable storage devices include floppy drives, tape-backup drives, and Zip or Jaz disk drives.

 Many older PCs include a floppy disk drive that holds 3.5-inch diskettes; however, many newer PCs do not come standard with such disk drives.

The storage capacity of these devices is measured in bytes. A byte is a collection of eight binary digits or bits, where each bit must either be a 1 or a 0. Each byte can represent a single character, number, or symbol. A kilobyte (KB) is 1,024 bytes and equals about one printed page of double-spaced text. A megabyte (MB) is 1,024 kilobytes, or just over one million bytes, and equals about one normal-sized paperback book. A gigabyte (GB) is 1,024 megabytes, or just over one billion bytes, and equals about six full sets of encyclopedias (see Figure 1-16). Table 1-1 compares the byte capacities of common storage devices.

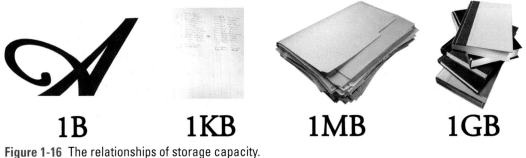

1B   1KB   1MB   1GB

Figure 1-16 The relationships of storage capacity.

Table 1-1 Common storage devices.

STORAGE DEVICE	DISK CAPACITY	USES
Hard drive	Varies, 20 GB to 140 GB or more	Store operating system, programs, and data files
Floppy drive	1.44 MB	Store small data files
CD drive	600 to 700 MB	Distribute software, backup personal data
DVD drive	4.7 to 17 GB	Distribute movies, backup personal data
Flash drive	Varies, 32 MB to 1 GB	Backup personal data

Hard Drive

A hard drive, as shown in Figure 1-17, is the most common PC storage device. It's typically located inside the system unit. The hard disk stores both the instructions and data the computer needs to run. Most hard drives offer capacities in the gigabyte range. Today's PCs typically feature large hard drives to enable users to store multimedia content in the form of MP3s, videos, and photos. These types of files require more hard drive space than simple word-processing documents or spreadsheets; hence, extra capacity is essential.

In general, a hard drive offers faster access to data than does any other storage device except RAM. But, unlike RAM, hard drive storage is permanent. Anything stored on a hard drive remains there until it's deleted.

Figure 1-17 A hard drive.

1

> **More About . . . Hard Drives**
>
> Hard drive space is precious—especially when you run short of room! Fortunately, you can easily upgrade your PC's storage by adding another drive to your machine. (Most PCs support at least two and as many as four hard drives. The first hard drive in a system is typically assigned drive letter C: by default. If another hard drive is present in a PC, it is assigned a subsequent letter.)
>
> Unless your PC supports only one hard drive, adding a second drive is preferable to replacing the existing one; that's because when you replace a hard drive, you must reinstall the operating system and other software and restore all your personal data. (If you must replace an existing drive, consider hiring a professional to migrate your software and data files for you. It could save you time and unnecessary heartache.)

Floppy Drive

A floppy drive reads information and writes information to 3.5-inch diskettes or floppy disks (see Figure 1-18). A typical floppy disk holds 1.44 MB of data, which by today's standards is quite small. Floppies can be used to transfer small files between two PCs; however, both PCs must have a floppy disk drive. Many newer computers do not have a floppy disk drive as standard equipment, although you can still purchase and install them if needed.

Figure 1-18 3 1/2-inch floppy disks.

CD and DVD Drives

When we first began using PCs, their main role was as a word processor, which was mainly characters and only used small amounts of data space. As time went on, we started adding visual support to our documents in the form of graphics, animation, and sound. These changes created larger files which required larger data space. While our computer hard drives hold large amounts of information, we need a way to back up or transport the information to other computers.

Today's computers usually include a drive (called an optical drive) with large data saving capacity, which could be in the form of a CD or DVD drive. CD denotes Compact Disc and DVD stands for Digital Video Disc. Both CD and DVD drives come in a variety of formats, which include the ability to only read files; to read and write files; or to read, write, and re-write files.

CDs, as seen in Figure 1-19, hold approximately 700 MB of data, which is the equivalent of about 500 floppy disks. DVDs hold about 5.2 GB of data, which is about as much as 8 CDs. Newer, larger 9.4 GB or even 17 GB capacity DVDs are rapidly gaining in popularity.

Figure 1-19 A typical CD.

Some optical drives not only read data from discs but allow you to copy information from your computer to the disc. With a recordable CD or DVD drive (see Figure 1-20), you can back up files, such as images, music, or important data, to CDs or DVDs.

Figure 1-20 A CD-RW drive not installed in the system unit.

There are several types of optical drives; most of which are recordable:

◆ CD-ROM drives. A CD-ROM (short for compact disc read-only memory) drive can read data on CD-ROMs (or CDs, for short). The ROM in CD-ROM stands for read-only memory, meaning that unlike a floppy disk, which can be read and written to, a CD-ROM can only be read by your PC.

◆ CD-R drives. A CD-R drive (R for read) can read data from CD-ROM discs and write to CD-R discs. A CD-R disc is a CD that can have data saved on it, or be written to, only one time. Once written to, a CD-R becomes a CD-ROM.

◆ CD-RW drives. A CD-RW drive (RW for read-write) has the same capabilities as a CD-R drive, but you can also use it to record data to the same CD multiple times. You can even erase a CD and reuse it. To take advantage of these additional capabilities, you must use a special type of CD called a CD-RW.

✦ DVD-R drives. A DVD-R drive (R for read) can view DVDs such as movies or it can read data written on CDs, including CD-RW discs. DVD-R drives can only read data; they cannot write data to a DVD or CD.

✦ DVD-RW drives. Like the CD-RW drive, a DVD-RW drive (RW for read-write) can do everything a CD-R drive can, but you can also use it to record data to the same DVD multiple times, including erasing and reusing it.

Flash Drives

Removable flash drives, sometimes referred to as flash memory or jump drives, are a wonderful way to move data from place to place. These drives are small enough to put in your pocket (some are keychain size) and attach to any computer with a USB port. They can hold important documents, hundreds of digital photos, or hours of MP3 music files.

Flash drives contain upgradeable flash memory in the form of a removable media card. You can purchase extra flash media to put into the flash drive so as one becomes full, you simply pull it out and stick in another empty reusable memory stick. Flash memory is available in a variety of capacities, ranging from 32 MB to 1 GB, although larger capacities are being developed every day.

When you insert a flash drive into a USB port on your computer, Windows will instantly recognize the item and assign it a drive letter.

 Be careful! Because the average flash drive is small (about three inches long, one or two inches wide, and about three-quarters of an inch thick), it can be easy to lose.

Power Supply

The power supply provides electricity to most installed components, such as the motherboard, hard drive, CD/DVD drives, and so on. The PC's main power cable plugs into the power supply on the back of the system unit case. The connection port for the power cable is often located near a fan, which helps cool the power supply so it can function efficiently.

Discovering Other Types of Computers

Desktops aren't the only variety of PCs on the market. Two other types, notebook computers and personal data assistants (PDAs), are designed for users on the go.

Notebook Computers

A notebook computer (also called a notebook PC, laptop, or portable computer) is a fully functional personal computer that's about the size of a college textbook—or even smaller, as shown in Figure 1-21. A notebook computer has a built-in screen, keyboard, and pointing device. Its pointing device can be a touchpad, a small joystick, or a trackball, but all do the same thing as a standard mouse. A notebook's screen is built into the upper half of its case, which closes to cover and protect the keyboard.

Notebooks also typically include a floppy drive, PC Card slots, multiple ports, and built-in speakers. It can run on external power or an internal battery. Most new notebooks also include some type of CD or DVD drive. Notebooks offer many of the capabilities of a full-sized PC with the portability of a good book.

Figure 1-21 A notebook PC.

PDAs

A personal data assistant (PDA) is a portable computer that is designed to act as an organizer, note taker, communication device, and more (see Figure 1-22). A PDA is fast and functional. It also comes with a variety of user-friendly applications to help you quickly organize your business and personal activities.

Due to the small size of PDAs, they often possess the latest and most compact user interfaces with such features as touch screens, handwriting recognition, and miniature keyboards (both on-screen and attached to the device).

Figure 1-22 A personal data assistant.

CHAPTER 2

PC Connectors and Gadgets

There are a number of components that come with your computer, and it can be confusing figuring out how they all connect together. By understanding the cables and the places they plug into, called ports, you will be able to easily assemble your computer components or add new devices. A few of the most common peripherals or add-on devices include a mouse, monitor, or a printer.

Identifying Connection Types

Peripherals, also called add-on devices and/or external devices, are hardware devices that connect to a PC. Some peripherals are required, such as a keyboard, mouse, and monitor. Others are optional, such as a printer, digital camera, scanner, speaker, modem, and network interface card (also called NICs). To do its job, each peripheral must somehow connect to the PC itself.

Internal and external devices use a variety of connections to link to a system unit. Each connection invariably involves some kind of cable that uses one or more specific type of connector (sometimes, in fact, you'll find different types of connectors on each end of a cable). A basic understanding of connection types and connectors on your PC is helpful, because there's a good chance you'll want to add a peripheral at some point.

Before we discuss common PC peripherals in more detail, let's examine common connections and related connectors that you'll find both inside and outside your system unit.

Internal Connections

If the inside of your system unit is a mystery, this section will help you understand the connection types you see there. It will also help you when upgrading components, such as the memory.

Most internal connections are found directly on the motherboard, which is the fundamental component of any system unit. Figure 2-1 shows a typical motherboard; notice its various slots and connection points. Table 2-1 shows the connection types available on most motherboards.

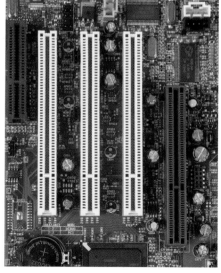

Figure 2-1 A typical motherboard.

Table 2-1 Internal connection types

Port	Common Uses
PCI	Sound cards, modems, or network NICs
AGP	Video cards
ATA/IDE	Hard drives, CD and DVD drives
Floppy	Floppy drives

Here are specifics for each of the connection types listed in Table 2-1:

✦ **PCI (Peripheral Component Interconnect).** The PCI slots are the most obvious connection points on the motherboard, as shown in Figure 2-2. Some motherboards have as few as two PCI slots, whereas others have as many as six.

✦ **AGP (Accelerated Graphics Port).** Another type of connection on the motherboard is the AGP port, which connects the video card. In most cases, an AGP port is brown in color and is located next to the PCI slots. Most motherboards have only one AGP port.

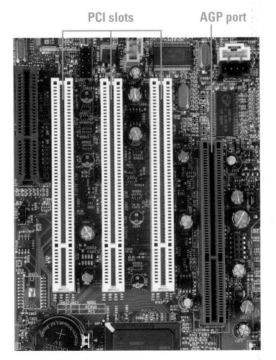

Figure 2-2 PCI slots and an AGP port.

✦ **ATA (Advanced Technology Attachment).** An ATA connection enables connections for Integrated Drive Electronics (IDE) hard drives (discussed shortly) and CD and DVD drives. An ATA ribbon cable connects one or two IDE drives to each ATA connection port. Most newer motherboards include two ATA connection ports (see Figure 2-3) for as many as four IDE drives.

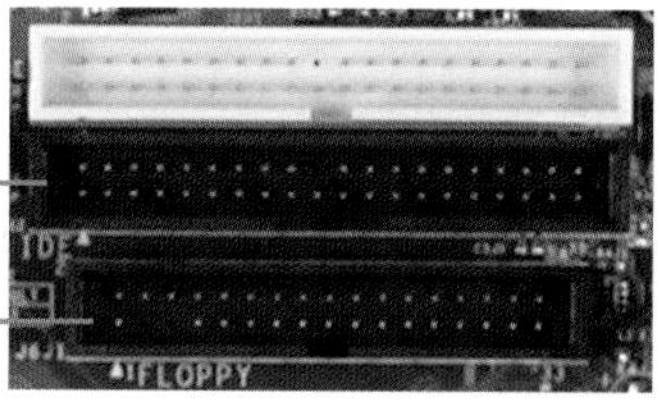

ATA connection ports

Figure 2-3 ATA connection ports on a motherboard.

You'll also find another connection on most motherboards; it's a bit shorter than the previously described ATA ports. This is the floppy-connection port. A floppy ribbon cable connects one or two floppy drives. Older PCs that included a floppy drive will connect to this port.

External Connections

The abundance of external connection ports exists to ensure you'll always have some way to connect your latest peripheral purchase to your PC. You use external ports to connect monitors, keyboards, mouse devices, printers, scanners, digital cameras, MP3 players, microphones, speakers, and so much more. All you need to determine is whether you have a free port of the correct connection type and the right cables to connect your devices to the system unit.

There is one important notion to keep in mind when connecting external devices— namely, gender. The connection cables, the system unit case ports, and the ports on the device itself all have a gender. For the most part, connectors with metal pins or connection points that protrude are male; those that are recessed are female. Ultimately, it doesn't matter how you label either one, as long as you have a matched set you can plug together. Table 2-2 shows the common external connection types. Figure 2-4 shows the back of a system unit and identifies locations for external connections.

Table 2-2 The common external connection types.

PORT	COMMON USES
Serial	Modems, label printers, mouse devices, PDAs, older digital cameras
Parallel	Printers
SVGA/VGA	Monitors
PS/2	Keyboards, mouse devices
USB	Mouse devices, keyboards, printers, label printers, digital cameras, music players, scanners, PDAs, CD/DVD drives, external hard drives, tape backups
IEEE 1394 FireWire®	Printers, digital cameras, digital video, music players, scanners, CD/DVD drives, tape backups
PC Card	NICs, modems, extra memory, digital-camera memory-card readers

Here are specifics for each of the connection types listed in Table 2-2:

+ **Serial.** Most PCs built today have one DB9-pin serial port, whereas older systems typically have one DB9 and one DB25 connector. Both types of serial ports on the system unit are male, and require a female cable to connect to external devices. In most cases, only a single device can be connected to each serial port.

PS/2
USB

VGA
Parallel
Serial

Microphone
and Speaker

Figure 2-4 The collection of external ports on the back of a system unit.

More About . . . Serial Ports

If you use external serial devices, you are bound to run into difficulty at some point in connecting them to your system. That's because serial ports on the back of your PC are always male, but the serial ports on devices can be either male or female. In addition to having different genders, there are two sizes for serial connectors: DB9 and DB25. To accommodate all possible combinations when connecting your serial devices, you may need to obtain the following:

+ A serial cable with a male DB9 connector at each end.

+ A serial cable with one male DB9 and one female DB9 connector.

+ A serial connector converter that has a female DB9 on one side and a male DB25 on the other.

+ A serial connector converter that has a male DB9 on one side and a female DB25 on the other.

✦ **Parallel.** The parallel port (also called a DB25 port) on the system unit is always female (see Figure 2-5). In most cases, only a single external device can be connected to a parallel port.

> Both parallel and the older, larger serial ports use the same DB25 connector type. However, serial and parallel ports are quite different types of connection interfaces. The parallel port on the system unit case is always female, and the two serial ports on the system unit case are always male.

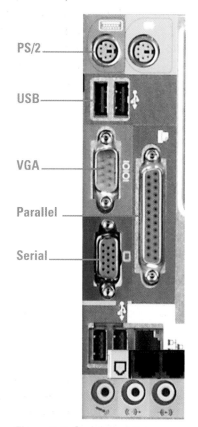

✦ **SVGA/VGA (Super VGA/Video Graphics Array).** Most modern video cards and monitors support SVGA, which is an enhanced version of VGA capable of improved display resolution and color depth. The SVGA/VGA port is the same size and shape as the small serial port, but has 15 pins instead of 9 (see Figure 2-5) and is female on the system unit.

✦ **PS/2.** Two female PS/2 ports are found on most desktop PCs (see Figure 2-5). One is reserved for the mouse, and the other for the keyboard. Most notebooks, on the other hand, have only a single PS/2 port, which can be used to attach either an external mouse or keyboard.

Figure 2-5 Serial, parallel, VGA, USB, and PS/2 ports.

◆ **USB (Universal Serial Bus).** USB connections (see Figure 2-6) allow faster response and take advantage of Windows XP's Plug and Play feature, which allows you to simply plug a peripheral into the USB port and use it immediately. The operating system automatically installs drivers for the peripheral (you may be prompted for the driver disk), and you'll rarely need to restart your PC. Although USB is usually seen in version 2.0, which offers very fast throughput speeds, some older PCs may only use the slower version 1.1.

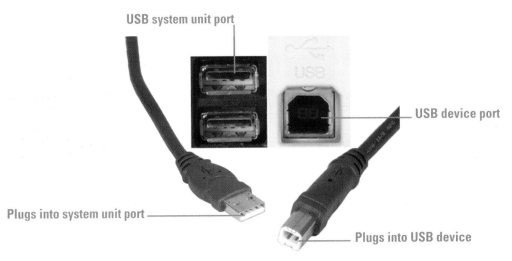

Figure 2-6 The ends of a USB cable and the USB ports on a system unit and a USB device.

The wide range of USB devices available includes keyboards, mouse devices, printers, hard drives, CD and DVD drives, digital cameras, scanners, PDAs, and tape-backup units. Some USB devices are powered, meaning they include external power supplies that must plug into a power strip or surge protector. Others, such as keyboards and mouse devices, are unpowered, meaning they draw power through the USB connection itself.

More About ... USB

Most new PCs have many USB ports—as many as 8. Some PCs have built-in USB ports on the front and some in the back. If you find yourself in need of additional USB ports, you need a USB hub, a device that transforms a single USB port into additional ports. In all, USB ports can be used to interconnect as many as 127 devices.

If multiple devices that draw power from the USB port are connected to a single USB port on the system unit via a USB hub, those devices may not receive sufficient power to operate properly (as a rule, no more than three unpowered USB devices should be connected to a single USB port on the system unit). To resolve this issue, a powered USB hub can be used to boost the power available to USB devices through the USB connection.

✦ **FireWire.** FireWire, also commonly referred to as IEEE1394 (see Figure 2-7), offers fast throughput and can support as many as 127 devices (the same as USB). FireWire is actually a trademark of Apple Computer and is part of the IEEE 1394 standard. PCs with built-in FireWire support usually have two ports in the back and at least one in the front. Some FireWire connections have six pins, like the one in Figure 2-7, while other connections use a smaller, 4-pin connection.

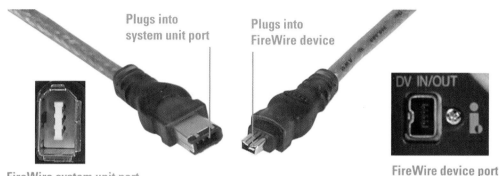

Plugs into system unit port

Plugs into FireWire device

DV IN/OUT

FireWire system unit port

FireWire device port

Figure 2-7 FireWire system unit port, cable ends, and device connector port.

More About . . . FireWire

FireWire is similar to USB in several ways:

    ✦ As many as 127 devices can be connected if you use hubs.

    ✦ Unpowered FireWire devices draw power from the connection.

    ✦ Powered FireWire devices have their own separate power supplies.

    ✦ The number of unpowered FireWire devices on a single port should be limited to three or fewer.

✦ **PC Card.** This connection type, once known as Personal Computer Memory Card International Association (PCMCIA), was renamed PC Card because it was used for more than memory cards. PC Card slots hold PC Cards. Although PC Cards are used mainly on notebooks, PC Card adapters are available for desktop PCs, which means you can use the same peripherals or interfaces with both desktop and notebook PCs.

Understanding Input Devices

Input devices are tools you use to get information from the world into your PC. You won't believe how many input devices have been developed for the PC; some of the most common include a mouse, keyboard, scanner, and digital camera.

Keyboards

A keyboard (see Figure 2-8) is probably the most familiar input device for a PC. You use the keyboard to enter numbers, letters, symbols, and even control commands into your PC. From the keyboard, you can control programs and input data. A keyboard is typically connected to a PC through a PS/2 or USB connection.

Figure 2-8 A typical keyboard.

More About . . . Keyboards

Simplicity and freedom from cables come in the form of a wireless keyboard. A wireless keyboard communicates with your computer via radio signals. Setup typically requires installing some software and plugging a radio receiver into a USB port of the computer. With most wireless keyboards, the receiver and keyboard do not need to be pointed at each other like a TV remote. Rather, they need only be within about 30 feet of each other. The keyboards are powered by standard batteries, which typically last up to nine months.

For more information about keyboards, see Chapter 4.

The Mouse

The mouse (see Figure 2-9) is a small device that you use to move the mouse pointer on the screen. You use the buttons on a mouse to select options, buttons, or commands when the mouse pointer hovers over them. Some older mice have a ball underneath them that moves on a foam pad called a mouse pad, while the newer mice are optical and use a laser to detect the mouse movement. Optical mice have no mechanical moving parts and respond more quickly and precisely than mechanical mice. A mouse is typically connected to the PC through a serial, PS/2, or USB connection.

Figure 2-9 An optical mouse.

More About . . . Mouse Devices

There are several alternatives to the common mouse seen in Figure 2-9, including trackballs, wireless mice (see Figure 2-10), touchpads, graphical tablets, and mouse sticks. You'll learn more about mouse devices in Chapter 4.

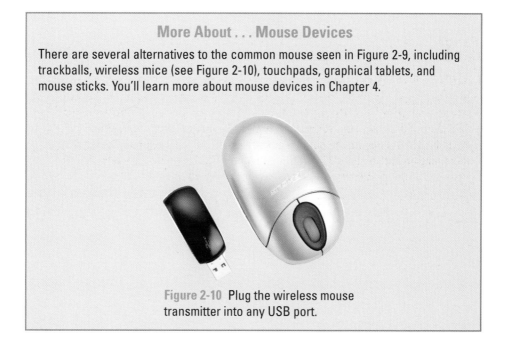

Figure 2-10 Plug the wireless mouse transmitter into any USB port.

Scanners

A scanner is a device that converts just about any image—from slides or photos to transparencies, graphics, or even text—into digital form. A scanner (shown in Figure 2-11) usually includes software that can then be used to capture, print, or transfer the image. Some scanners also provide fax and copy functions at the touch of a button. After you scan an image and save it to a file, you can do many things with it. For example, you can e-mail it to friends or make it your desktop wallpaper. A scanner is typically connected to a PC through a USB or FireWire connection.

Figure 2-11 A typical scanner.

 Some high-end scanners include a feature called Optical Character Recognition (OCR), allowing a scanned text image to be converted into an object that a word-processing application understands.

Digital Cameras

Digital cameras photograph still or, in some cases, video digital images that can be fed directly into your PC. Unlike regular cameras, digital cameras (see Figure 2-12) don't use film; instead, they store images on memory cards or rewritable optical disks. A digital image is just like any other image in your PC. You can edit, print, view, or send them to others via e-mail, or even post them to Web sites. A digital camera is typically connected to a PC through a USB or FireWire connection.

Figure 2-12 A typical digital camera.

Working with Output Devices

An output device is any hardware component that produces something you can touch, see, or hear. There are too many output devices to name them all, but some of the most common include monitors, printers, speakers, and MP3 players.

Monitors

A monitor, which looks a lot like a television screen, displays visual output for a PC (see Figure 2-13). With a monitor, you can see your documents, view pictures, watch movies, and interact with your PC's operating system (you'll learn more about performing such actions later). Monitors come in a wide range of sizes, from 15 to 21 inches (this measurement reflects the length of the diagonal from one corner to the other); the larger the display area, the more detail you can see on the screen. Typically, monitors connect to a PC through a VGA connection on a video card (you should note that a high-end monitor requires a high-end video card to produce acceptable images on your screen).

Figure 2-13 A flat panel monitor.

There are two major types of PC monitors available today:

✦ **Tube monitors.** A tube monitor looks like a television set—heavy, large, and boxy. The size and weight of a tube monitor comes from its core component: a glass cathode ray tube (CRT).

✦ **Flat panel monitors.** Flat panel monitors are narrow in profile in comparison with tube monitors, and provide crisp, clean images that are more vibrant and brilliant than some tube monitors. For this reason, flat panel monitors are usually more expensive than a tube monitor of the same size.

The improved display of flat panel monitors stems from its flat, pixel-based display (not a projection onto a curved surface, as with a CRT). The size of both tube and flat panel monitors is a measurement of the diagonal distance from one corner across the screen to the opposite corner. The viewable area is typically less on a tube monitor versus a flat panel.

Although the term "monitor" can apply to a tube or a flat panel monitor, this term occurs more often when discussing tube monitors. When flat panel monitors are mentioned, they are often called "flat screens or flat panel" rather than "monitors." The term "LCD monitor" is also common, but is technically incorrect. Most new flat panel monitors use a type of technology that differs from LCD (Liquid Crystal Display).

> ### More About . . . Monitors
>
> A monitor's quality is usually rated in the density of its display and its refresh rate. A monitor's density is rated in dot pitch in millimeters (mm) and indicates how closely the points of color are packed together. Dot pitch is the distance between points of color on a monitor screen. The better the monitor's display, the lower its dot-pitch rating. A rating of 0.22 is fairly good. A monitor's refresh rate is how often the displayed image is re-drawn. In tube monitors, refresh rate is rated in hertz (Hz) (re-draws per second), where a larger number indicates better quality. A refresh rate of 85 Hz is fairly good. A flat panel monitor's refresh rate, on the other hand, is rated in response time in milliseconds (ms), where a smaller number indicates better quality. A response time of 30 ms is fairly good.

Printers

A printer is a device that prints text or graphical images from your computer on paper (see Figure 2-14). Printers can produce black or color output. Most printers use standard paper, but some can print on transparency film, slide film, drafting paper, and photo paper, as well as labels and envelopes. A printer is typically connected to a PC through a parallel or USB connection.

Figure 2-14 An inkjet printer.

There are two main types of printers:

- ✦ **Inkjet.** Inkjet printers produce output by spraying microscopic drops of ink onto the paper as it passes through the printer. Most inkjet printers can print both color and black images, but sometimes the ink can smear or bleed. Inkjets are fairly inexpensive, but they print slowly in comparison with laser printers.

- ✦ **Laser.** Laser printers produce output by using a system of lasers to adhere and bond a powdered toner onto paper. Laser printers produce detailed high-quality images, and laser printer output rarely smears. Some laser printers can print color images, but most produce only black text on white paper, or grayscale images. Laser printers are usually more than twice the price of a comparable inkjet printer, but they produce much more detailed output at a much faster rate.

In addition to inkjet and laser printers, there are also many types of specialty printers on the market, such as label printers, photo printers, plotters, and slide printers. These printers handle unique output media that a typical inkjet or laser printer is sometimes unable to handle efficiently, if at all.

More About . . . Printers

When purchasing a printer, it's important to shop around and compare features. The challenge is, every printer company describes a printer's capabilities using different terminology and ranking methods. To make a meaningful comparison, find a computer store with multiple printers on display so you can print on each one. Without side-by-side comparison of the same document from multiple devices, you can't tell which printer actually produces higher-quality output.

Also, realize that the most-expensive printer is not always the best printer. Printers often offer features or capabilities that home users don't need or want. Many such features, such as an extra large-capacity auto-feed paper tray or a sorting attachment, dramatically increase prices. Look for models that provide the features you need without too many unwanted features.

Speakers

Speakers produce audio output from a PC (see Figure 2-15). Through speakers or a set of headphones, you can hear operating-system sounds, music, sound effects from games, or the soundtracks of DVDs. Speakers are typically connected to a PC's sound card using one or more ⅛-inch stereo jack(s), the same type of connector at the end of the headphones you use on your portable radio or CD player.

Figure 2-15 Common speakers.

MP3 Players

An MP3 player (see Figure 2-16) is a portable device that plays digitally recorded music. MP3 players have either a large amount of memory or a hard drive on which digital music is stored. Once you transfer music from a PC to the player, you can use the player anywhere to listen to your favorite tunes. MP3 players may typically be attached to a PC using a serial, USB, or FireWire connection (the faster the connection, the quicker it will be to download music to your player from your PC).

Figure 2-16 An MP3 player.

More About . . . Audio Components

A PC can come to life if you take advantage of a sound card and speakers. You can listen to CDs or music from the Internet. You can get lost in the audio worlds created by PC games. With a portable MP3 player, you can even carry your favorite tunes with you wherever you go.

Most new PCs include a sound card and speakers of some kind. In addition, some of the most popular digital gadgets include portable MP3 players.

Discovering Communication Devices

Some types of hardware, such as modems and NICs, allow two or more PCs to communicate. These are called communication devices. The communication devices described in this section connect to expansion cards installed inside the system unit, or to an external serial, USB, FireWire, PC Card, or network interface card (NIC) connections.

More About . . . PC Communications

The ability to link your computer to other systems, especially to the Internet, opens up whole new worlds to explore. You can't imagine how much information is out there just waiting for you to discover. A PC with a communication device, such as a modem, can be easily connected to the Internet. For more information about connecting to and using the Internet, see Chapter 10.

Modems

A modem is a device that allows a PC to communicate with other PCs. There are three main types of modems: voice modem, cable modem, and DSL modem. Voice modems use a card installed inside the system unit (see Figure 2-17) which then connects to a standard phone line. Some voice modems are an external device connected to a PC via a serial cable. Voice modems offer maximum throughput of 56 Kbps.

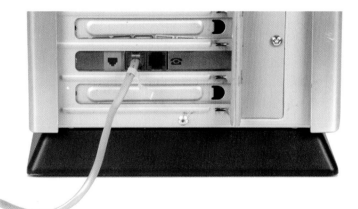

Figure 2-17 A expansion-card modem with connected phone cord.

 A new kid is arriving on the block. High-speed satellite modems, like satellite dishes, rely on communication through a satellite up in space.

Cable Modems

A cable modem (see Figure 2-18) is used to connect to a high-speed broadband Internet service. Many cable-television companies offer this type of service. Cable Internet service typically offers up to 2 Mbps for downloads and 300 Kbps for uploading data. Cable Internet service is a shared medium, however, which means that if many people in your neighborhood use their cable modem connections at the same time, everyone's connection runs slower. Cable modems are typically external devices that connect to a PC through a NIC.

Figure 2-18 A cable modem.

DSL Modems

DSL (digital subscriber line) modems (see Figure 2-19) use a new feature of digital

telephone service to provide high-speed Internet access. DSL requires that the telephone company deploy specific hardware in your area; in addition, your house must be located within a specific distance from the switching station where DSL access is made available to local subscribers.

Figure 2-19 A DSL modem.

A DSL connection uses your phone line, but allows you to place and receive calls while also connected to the Internet. DSL connections typically offer 384 Kbps to 1.5 Mbps download and 128 Kbps upload throughput. The real benefit of DSL is that it's a dedicated medium. In other words, the presence of other DSL users in your neighborhood won't affect your upload and download speeds. DSL modems are either expansion cards installed inside the system unit or external devices connected to a NIC.

NICs

A PC connects to a network using a NIC, short for network interface card (see Figure 2-20). A network allows multiple PCs to share files, printers, data, and even Internet connections. A NIC permits a PC to attach to a network, through which you can connect to the Internet as well. A PCI NIC is an internal expansion card that gets installed inside the system unit case onto the motherboard by attaching to a PCI slot. A PC Card NIC is an expansion card about the size of a credit card that slips into a PC Card slot on the side of a notebook PC.

Figure 2-20 A PCI NIC and a PC Card NIC.

Reviewing Power Devices

Your PC needs electricity to operate, but providing electricity introduces certain risks. The electricity that powers our homes and offices is not as reliable and consistent as we might like. The electric company, other houses in the neighborhood, and appliances within your own home can cause minor fluctuations in the flow of electricity—for example, you've probably seen your lights dim when your air conditioner or refrigerator turns on.

At least three peripheral devices—surge protectors, UPSs, and static guards—can prevent electricity from damaging your PC system.

Surge Protectors

A surge protector (see Figure 2-21) is both a power-outlet multiplier and an electric-spike protector. An absolute must for any electronic device, especially a PC, a surge protector includes a fuse or built-in circuit breaker that disconnects power if a spike occurs. This protects your system from electric-spike damage, but the sudden loss of power might cause you to lose unsaved data.

Figure 2-21 A surge protector.

 Be sure to select a surge protector that has a guarantee and warranty.

UPSs

A UPS (uninterruptible power supply) is a battery and power conditioner for your PC (see Figure 2-22). A UPS connects between the wall outlet and your PC. It conditions electricity so your PC is fed only clean, consistent power. If the electricity fails, a UPS can continue to supply a PC with power from the battery. The

Figure 2-22 An uninterruptible power supply.

length of time a UPS can provide battery power depends on its battery size and the amount of power that the attached devices draw. In most cases, a UPS provides at least 10 minutes of emergency power. This provides ample time to perform a clean "shutdown" on a running system before the power is exhausted.

A UPS should be purchased for any system that must remain operative even during a power failure, or if you don't want to risk having your power instantly terminated by a surge protector. Be sure to purchase a UPS that supports your PC for at least 10 minutes.

Anti-Static Devices

Figure 2-23 An anti-static device.

Anti-static devices (see Figure 2-23) channel static electricity from your body to a safe ground. These devices can be wristbands, ankle bands, or desktop mats, and typically connect to the ground screw in a power outlet. They work only when you touch the static guard before touching any PC equipment. In many cases, true protection persists only if you remain in contact with the static guard throughout the entire time you are touching the PC. If you often shock yourself on doorknobs or other people, this peripheral is a must for you!

Unfortunately, even a minor power spike can damage a PC. Under some circumstances—such as when you might open your system unit and handle internal PC components or the motherboard—the sensitive electronics within a PC may not withstand even a small spark of static electricity.

Let's Get Started!

N ow that you know about the components that make up a typical PC, let's get you up and running. In this chapter, you'll connect your PC's components, use Windows XP's initial setup wizard to install and configure the operating system, and activate and register your copy of Windows XP. You'll then review the process of setting up your printer, so you can print those pictures of your family and friends to post on the refrigerator.

Getting Started

If you've just received your PC, unpack all its components and check them against your packing slip to make sure everything's on hand. At a minimum, you should have a system unit, monitor, keyboard, and mouse. You may also have speakers and a printer, as well as additional devices that need to be connected.

Once you've unpacked your PC, it's time to put it together and make sure it's working. Your Gateway PC shipped with a step-by-step guide that explains how to connect all of the components, along with helpful text and diagrams; refer to that for specifics on putting together your machine.

System unit case (tower)

Monitor

Speakers

To supplement the information that came with your PC, we've provided a step-by-step guide to putting your PC together. These steps assume you have a system unit, monitor, keyboard, mouse, set of speakers, and surge protector. Before you start, place your monitor on your desk. The closer it is to eye level when you sit at your desk, the better you'll like its location. Next, set the system case either next to the monitor or on the floor under your desk.

The cords and cables used to connect the devices help determine how far away the system unit can be placed. In general, they should be less than four feet apart.

Printer

Mouse

Surge protector

Keyboard

Then, plug all of the components together and hook up to a power source:

1 Plug the mouse cable into the appropriate port on the back of the system unit, as shown in Figure 3-1. If you have a mouse pad, place it under the mouse.

2 Plug the keyboard cable into the appropriate port on the back of the system unit case, as shown in Figure 3-1.

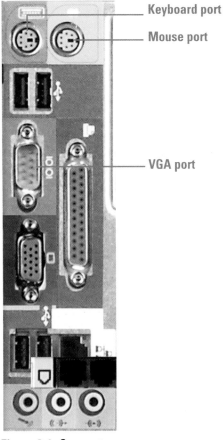

Keyboard port

Mouse port

VGA port

3 Locate the monitor cable (some monitor cables are directly connected to the monitor itself), and plug it into the VGA connector on the back of the system unit, as shown in Figure 3-1. If your monitor cable is not directly attached to the monitor, attach the proper end to the monitor.

Figure 3-1 Connect your mouse, keyboard, and monitor to your PC.

Surge protector

4 Connect the power cable to the monitor by plugging it into the back of the monitor, and then plugging it into a surge protector.

⑤ If your PC has a modem, connect a phone cable between the line jack on the system unit case and the appropriate wall jack. (If your surge protector also has phone line protection, hook it up as explained in the surge protector's directions.)

⑥ If your PC has speakers, connect them as instructed in the speaker setup guide.

⑦ Plug the speaker power supply into the speaker and into the surge protector or power strip.

 Some speaker sets include a separate power cable for each speaker, while others include a subwoofer and multiple satellite speakers. Consult your speaker user manual for proper connections and positioning.

⑧ Connect the power cable for the system unit by plugging the cable into the back of the system unit and then plugging it into the surge protector.

> **More About ... Connecting Other Devices**
>
> At this point, you should have all the essential components of your PC connected, with the exception of your printer (covered in the "Setting Up Your Printer" section later in this chapter). That's not to say, however, that you can't add other peripherals to your PC. Many PC companies bundle with their PCs or sell separately a wide variety of peripherals, such as microphones, digital cameras, scanners, label printers, and music players.
>
> We cannot cover them all in this book; however, you can review the setup guide that came with each of your peripherals.

Powering Up Your PC

At this point, your PC is properly connected and ready to be turned on. Here are the steps you should take to turn on, or power up, your PC:

❶ For each device that has a power cable, locate its power or on/off button. The system unit's power switch is usually on the front.

❷ Turn on the surge protector.

❸ Turn on the monitor. This usually involves pressing a button on the lower front, or just under the front edge, of the monitor. When powered up, most monitors display a small green or amber light next to the power button.

An amber light indicates the monitor has power. A green light indicates that the monitor has power and the PC is sending a video signal to the monitor. If you follow these instructions, your monitor power light will be amber at this point.

❹ Turn on your speakers. Some speakers have switches in the front, whereas others have them on the back or sides. Sometimes the volume knob also acts as the on/off switch. Set the volume to about 30 percent of its maximum. When your computer starts up, you'll hear music and sounds; you can adjust the volume then.

❺ If you have a printer already connected, turn it on. If you don't have a printer, or your printer is not yet connected, skip this step. We discuss printer connection later in this chapter.

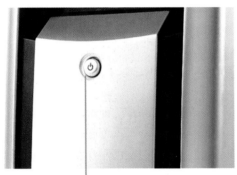

❻ Press the power button on the system unit.

Power button

After powering up, your PC performs a built-in power-on self test (POST) routine. This test inspects the PC's basic parts and makes sure they're present and working. You might also see some text and numbers, as well as lists of devices and settings, on the monitor during this phase. Then, the PC begins to load an operating system, also referred to as an OS. If all goes well, the icon and name of your operating system is displayed on the monitor; when the operating system is fully loaded, a first-time setup screen appears.

More About . . . Booting

Although PCs usually boot from an internally installed hard drive, some older PCs may try and boot first from a floppy disk. If you have a floppy drive on your PC and a non-bootable floppy is found in the floppy drive, then the PC will issue an error. Remove the floppy disk and press the ENTER key to continue booting from the computer hard drive.

Using The Windows XP Setup Wizard

The first time you start up your PC, a special Welcome screen appears, and if your speakers are hooked up, you'll probably hear music as well. This screen is the first screen of Windows XP's initial setup wizard, which asks you a series of questions in order to customize and complete your operating system installation.

Depending on how your version of Windows was installed, Windows XP may prompt you for a product key—a string of numbers and letters, organized into groups—to verify that you are the system's valid owner, and thus prevent software theft. You'll find the Windows product key on a sticker on one of the booklets included with your computer.

During the initial setup process, you will be prompted for the following information (look for system-specific instructions included with your PC for more information about this process):

✦ **Speakers.** Windows XP will ask you if your speakers are working and provides several opportunities on the screen to reconnect them and test them if they are not functioning correctly.

✦ **Time zone.** You define your time zone to enable your PC's system clock to track time properly given your geographic location. Select your time zone from the drop-down list, and be sure to indicate whether your area uses Daylight Savings Time.

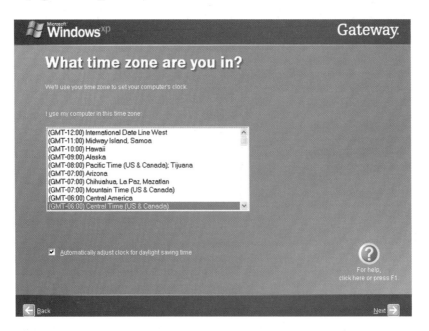

✦ **End User License Agreements (EULA).** This document protects Microsoft's and Gateways legal interests in developing and selling software and hardware. You must agree to the terms of both agreements before you can complete the setup process.

✦ **Computer name.** Every computer must have a name—preferably something descriptive. For example, you could name your PC after its primary user (you) or its location, such as "TomDesktop" or "LibraryPC." The name can be as many as 15 characters long and can use any combination of letters, numbers and hyphens but no spaces are allowed.

✦ **User name.** Windows XP employs user accounts to manage and control who can access the system. You are prompted to define at least one user account by specifying a user name during the initial setup process. A user name can be anything you like, as long as it contains 20 or fewer characters.

✦ **Internet connection.** Windows XP prompts you to configure an Internet connection during initial setup, and provides a number of different options for selecting an Internet Service Provider (ISP) if you don't already have one.

Once you've completed the initial setup process, the system completes the boot cycle, logs in to the user account you defined during setup, and presents you with the Windows XP desktop. The initial setup routine is a one-time process that does not occur again; the next time your system starts, it takes you directly to your desktop. Now that setup is complete, you have 30 days to activate the Windows XP software, as covered in the next section.

Activating and Registering Windows XP

We mentioned earlier that Windows XP requires you to enter a product key in order to prevent software theft. To this end, Microsoft requires you to activate your copy of Windows XP within 30 days of installation on your PC and requests that you register your copy of Windows XP as well.

Why Activate?

To combat software piracy in the form of casual copying and hard-drive cloning, Microsoft requires you to activate your copy of Windows XP within 30 days of installing it. Don't let activation scare you; it's quick, simple, and protects your privacy—and may even help keep software prices down in the future.

 If you fail to activate your copy of Windows within 30 days of installing it, your system will start but you will not be able to use Windows XP or any other installed software until you complete the activation process.

When you activate your copy of Windows XP, a digital system ID unique to your PC is created. This digital system ID is like your social security number. Each hardware component in your PC is encoded with a unique ID; Windows XP takes the IDs from 10 devices or components within your PC and uses them to create a system ID.

 If you change more than six components within your system, its digital ID may change. If that happens, your activation will be revoked. Don't worry. You need only call Microsoft to tell them you upgraded your machine. They'll help you resolve your activation problem by phone. The phone number is the same one you will call for initial activation, as covered in the "Activating and Registering Online or By Phone" section later in this chapter.

During activation, this system ID and your product key are recorded in a database of valid users at Microsoft. If someone else installs your copy of Windows XP software and attempts to activate his or her system, the system ID for the new system won't match the system ID for the old system, but the same product key will appear twice. This informs Microsoft that a piracy attempt is underway and that the second activation should be denied.

 During the process of activation, no personal information is sent to Microsoft.

To avoid inadvertently becoming a software pirate yourself, you should purchase a separate copy of each program and operating system for every PC you own. Such software is often included as a part of a PC purchase.

Why Register?

Unlike activation, registering your copy of Windows XP is optional. Doing so, however, helps establish your rights as an end user and software purchaser. It ensures that you can access technical support and, if necessary, make claims against the software's warranty and

End User License Agreement (EULA). You'll also become eligible to receive informational e-mail and postal mail from Microsoft.

Activating and Registering Online or By Phone

Although you can activate your copy of Windows XP via phone, it's much easier to do so online. Using the Internet to activate your PC takes less than two minutes and enables you to register with Microsoft at the same time.

To activate over the Internet, follow these steps:

1 Click the **start** button (the green button in the lower-left corner of your desktop), point to **All Programs**, point to **Accessories**, point to **System Tools**, and then click **Activate Windows**.

① **Activate Windows**

Let's activate Windows

To help reduce software piracy, please activate your copy of Windows now. Activation over the Internet is quick and easy.

You don't need to give your name or other personal information when you activate Windows.

Do you want to activate Windows now?

- ● <u>Y</u>es, let's activate Windows over the Internet now
- ● Yes, I want to <u>t</u>elephone a customer service representative to activate Windows
- ● N<u>o</u>, remind me to activate Windows every few days

If you wait to activate, you can still use Windows, but you will receive periodic reminders. After 60 day(s), you must activate Windows before you can continue to use it.

Microsoft is committed to your privacy. For more information, <u>read the Windows Product Activation Privacy Statement</u>

To continue, click Next.

[<u>N</u>ext]

2 The Let's activate Windows screen appears. Click the Yes, let's activate Windows over the Internet now option, and then click Next.

3 The Register with Microsoft? screen appears. If you want to register, click the Yes option. If you don't want to register, click the No option. Click Next to continue.

4 If you selected Yes, the Collecting registration data screen appears. Type your name, address, city, state, zip, country, and e-mail address in the fields provided. You can also click the various check boxes to receive promotional materials from Microsoft and Microsoft partners. Click Next.

5 Windows XP contacts Microsoft over the Internet and performs the activation. After a few moments, the Thank you screen appears. Click Finish.

If you don't have Internet access or prefer the phone method, follow these steps:

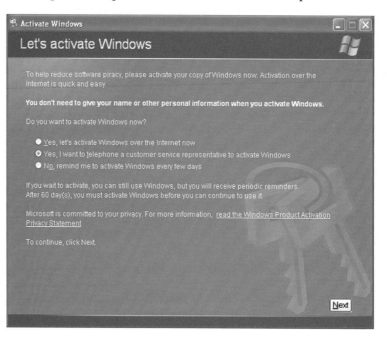

① Click the **start** button (the green button in the lower-left corner of your desktop), point to **All Programs**, point to **Accessories**, point to **System Tools**, and then click **Activate Windows**.

② The Let's activate Windows screen appears. Click the **Yes, I want to telephone a customer service representative to activate Windows** option, and click **Next**.

③ The Activate Windows by phone screen appears. In the section labeled "Step 1," click the drop-down arrow to select your geographical location. All the world's countries appear in alphabetical order. Click your country.

④ The phone number you should call to activate your copy of Windows XP appears in the section labeled "Step 2." Use a telephone to call this number.

⑤ Follow the instructions the customer service representative (CSR) gives you. Usually, he or she asks for the system ID displayed in section labeled "Step 3" on your screen.

⑥ The CSR provides you with a 42-digit confirmation ID. In the section labeled "Step 4" on your screen, type this ID in the boxes under the letters A through G.

⑦ After you type the confirmation ID, click Next. If any problems occur, talk to the CSR to resolve them.

⑧ Click Finish. You are finished activating Windows XP over the phone.

If you activate your copy of Windows XP over the phone, you are not given the opportunity to register with Microsoft at the same time. In this case, you may complete the product registration card included with your Windows XP software and mail it to Microsoft.

Now that you've set up your computer and operating system, you'll want to set up your printer.

Setting Up Your Printer

Once you've unpacked your printer and positioned it in its new home on your desk, setting it up to print is simple. In fact, the process is often entirely automatic after you connect the printer's cables to the system unit.

 Before you connect your printer, it's a good idea to follow the basic setup as defined in the printer's setup manual. This includes installing an ink or toner cartridge and filling the paper tray.

Connecting the Printer

To connect a printer to your PC, follow these steps:

① Plug the larger end of the printer cable into the back of the printer.

 Most printers do not include a printer cable; it must be purchased separately.

② Plug the other end of the printer cable into the appropriate port—USB or parallel—on the back of your system unit. (Chapter 2 explains the differences between USB and parallel ports and cables.)

③ Plug one end of the printer's power cable into the printer.

④ Plug the other end of the printer's power cable into the surge protector.

⑤ Turn the printer on.

If you have a USB printer, Windows XP may detect it automatically and start the installation process by itself. If so, follow whatever on-screen prompts appear. For example, you may be asked to verify the installation, or to provide a driver disk (often a CD-ROM) if Windows XP doesn't have the necessary drivers pre-loaded. (Device drivers are discussed in Chapter 1.) In most cases, the driver disk is included with the printer.

Manually Installing the Printer

If Windows XP does not automatically detect and install your printer after you connect it to your PC, you can install the printer manually. Follow these steps:

❶ Click the **start** button, and then click **Printers and Faxes**.

 If you don't see a Printers and Faxes icon in the start menu, you can access it by clicking **start**, then **Control Panel**, then **Printers and Other Hardware**, and then **Printers and Faxes**.

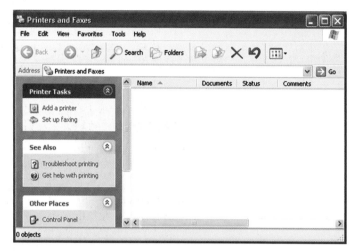

❷ The Printers and Faxes window opens. Click the **Add a printer** option in the Printer Tasks area.

❸ The Add Printer wizard starts, displaying the Welcome to the Add Printer Wizard screen. Click **Next**.

❹ The Local or Network Printer screen of the Add Printer wizard appears. Here, you indicate whether the printer is connected directly to your PC (that is, locally) or is connected to your machine via a network. These steps assume the printer is connected locally. Click the **Local printer attached to this computer** option button, and under that, select the **Automatically detect and install my Plug and Play printer** check box. Click **Next**.

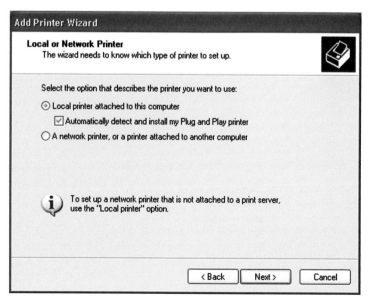

5 The New Printer Detection screen appears as the Add Printer wizard attempts to detect your printer automatically. If the wizard detects your printer, click Next and skip to step 13. If not, you'll have to complete the installation manually; click Next and continue to step 6.

6 In the Select a Printer Port screen, use the selection that appears automatically in the **Use the following port** list or select the port to which your printer is attached. (A parallel port printer is connected to LPT1, whereas a USB printer is connected to a USB port.) Click Next.

Add Printer Wizard

Select a Printer Port
Computers communicate with printers through ports.

Select the port you want your printer to use. If the port is not listed, you can create a new port.

⊙ Use the following port: LPT1: (Recommended Printer Port)   ▾

Note: Most computers use the LPT1: port to communicate with a local printer. The connector for this port should look something like this:

○ Create a new port:
   Type of port: Local Port   ▾

[< Back] [Next >] [Cancel]

7 Select the manufacturer of your printer in the left column of the Install Printer Software screen.

Add Printer Wizard

Install Printer Software
The manufacturer and model determine which printer software to use.

Select the manufacturer and model of your printer. If your printer came with an installation disk, click Have Disk. If your printer is not listed, consult your printer documentation for compatible printer software.

Manufacturer	Printers
Fujitsu	HP DraftPro Plus (C3170A)
GCC	HP DraftPro Plus (C3171A)
Generic	HP LaserJet 1100 (MS)
Gestetner	HP LaserJet 1200 Series PCL
HP	

This driver is digitally signed.   [Windows Update] [Have Disk...]
Tell me why driver signing is important

[< Back] [Next >] [Cancel]

8 If your printer is listed in the right column of the Install Printer Software screen, select it, click Next, and skip to step 13. If not, click the Have Disk button and continue to step 9.

⑨ The Install From Disk dialog box opens. Insert the printer vendor-supplied driver CD or floppy disk into the appropriate drive, and click the **Browse** button in the Install From Disk dialog box.

⑩ In the Locate File dialog box, click the **Look in** drop-down arrow and select the drive used in step 9.

⑪ Click **Open**. The setup tool scans the selected drive and displays a list of discovered drivers.

Add Printer Wizard

Name Your Printer
You must assign a name to this printer.

Type a name for this printer. Because some programs do not support printer and server name combinations of more than 31 characters, it is best to keep the name as short as possible.

Printer name:

HP LaserJet 1200 Series PCL

Do you want to use this printer as the default printer?

⊙ Yes
○ No

[< Back] [Next >] [Cancel]

⑫ Select the driver that matches your printer model. Click OK.

⑬ The Name Your Printer screen appears. Type a descriptive name for the printer, or accept the suggested name that is provided, and click Next.

⑭ The Print Test Page screen appears. Select Yes to print a test page, and click Next.

Add Printer Wizard

Completing the Add Printer Wizard

You have successfully completed the Add Printer Wizard. You specified the following printer settings:

Name: HP LaserJet 1200 Series PCL
Share name: <Not Shared>
Port: LPT1:
Model: HP LaserJet 1200 Series PCL
Default: Yes
Test page: No

To close this wizard, click Finish.

[< Back] [Finish] [Cancel]

⑮ The Completing the Add Printer Wizard screen appears. Click Finish.

At this point, Windows XP installs the printer driver, configures the printer, and prints a test page. After the test page prints successfully (and it will nine times out of 10), return to your PC and click OK when prompted.

Understanding the Desktop

After you turn on your computer and log on, you see Windows XP's computing environment, known as the desktop, depicted in Figure 3-2. The Windows XP desktop serves as a starting point for your computer session. You can open folders and documents and view them there, as well as access tools and other resources.

Figure 3-2 The default Windows XP desktop.

The desktop is so named because you use it in much the same way as you use the desk in your home or office: as a place to keep and access objects you are working on. Just as you might have a clock, folders, documents, and work-related tools on your physical desk, you can find the same sorts of computer tools on your Windows desktop.

An icon is a small graphic with a text label that represents an object or a shortcut to an object stored in another location. An object is anything in the computer system—such as a text document, music file, program, and so on—or anything attached to the PC, such as a printer, CD/DVD drive, floppy drive, hard drive, etc. You can access an object by clicking its icon; once an object is opened, or put in use, it typically appears within a window on the desktop.

The Recycle Bin

The Recycle Bin icon is the only icon that appears by default on a Windows XP desktop and is located in the lower-right corner. The Recycle Bin is a temporary storage location for recently deleted files, and you use it like the wastebasket beside your desk. If you

throw away a paper document and decide later you should keep it, you can always pull it out of the wastebasket—until you empty your trash, that is. Likewise, if you delete a file, you can recover it from the Recycle Bin until you tell Windows to empty it. The Recycle Bin is discussed further in Chapter 8.

3

The Taskbar

The taskbar, the colored strip that appears along the bottom of the screen, is a key component of the default Windows XP desktop. The taskbar helps you keep track of all the programs and documents open on your computer. When you start a program or open a window, a button representing that program or window appears in the taskbar. These buttons, called taskbar buttons, make it easy to switch between open windows or programs; you simply click a program's or window's button in the taskbar to switch to it. (You'll learn more about using taskbar buttons to switch programs and manage open windows in Chapter 5.) The two main features of the taskbar are the start button and the notification area.

Taskbar

The Start Button

You click the start button, located on the far-left side of the taskbar, to open the start menu. From the start menu, you can start programs, find documents, configure your computer, and much more.

Start button

The Notification Area

Located on the far-right side of the taskbar, the notification area displays small icons that represent programs that are running, but that do not appear on your desktop, such as anti-virus software. In addition, the notification area displays prompts when it needs to convey information about various system conditions, such as when your notebook computer is running on battery power, when an update is available for your operating system from Microsoft, when you have received an e-mail message, and so on.

![start button and taskbar with notification area at right showing icons and 3:45 PM]

Notification area

After seven days of inactivity, icons in the notification area become hidden. When any icons are hidden, a white arrow in a blue circle appears on the left edge of the notification area. Click the arrow to reveal these hidden icons; click the arrow again to hide them.

The clock appears in the notification area and displays the current time. Depending on your screen resolution and the customization of your taskbar, the day and the date may also be displayed. If you don't see the day and date, move your mouse pointer over the clock and leave it there for about two seconds. A ToolTip appears that names the day of the week, the month, the date, and the year.

![start button and taskbar with clock showing 3:45 PM]

Clock

Powering Down Your PC

When you're finished using your PC and want to turn it off, perform a shutdown. A shutdown is the action whereby Windows XP saves important data still contained in the memory, closes the desktop and operating system, and then powers off the PC. Shutdown is a process designed to prevent damage to your PC and to avoid data loss.

Never press the power button on your PC or pull the plug out of the wall without performing a shutdown first; otherwise, any data stored in memory not yet saved to disk will be lost. Plus, hard drives and other devices can be damaged if they lose power while operating. The shutdown process informs all components and attached peripherals that the PC is about to be turned off and instructs them to prepare for that event safely.

To shut down your PC, click the **start** button, and then click **Turn Off Computer**. The Turn off computer dialog box opens, as shown in Figure 3-3.

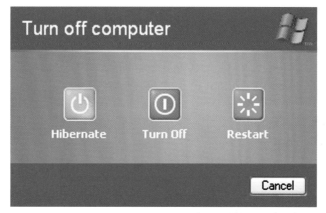

Figure 3-3 The Turn off computer dialog box.

Let's review the buttons in this dialog box:

✦ **Turn Off.** Click this button to save important data, close the operating system, and power down the PC.

 Some PCs automatically turn off their own power, whereas others display a screen informing you that it's safe to turn off the power.

✦ **Restart.** Click this button to restart the PC without losing power. This option is handy when you want to restart the system so it can load new drivers or use a new configuration setting.

✦ **Standby.** If standby is enabled, the left button is labeled "Standby." Click the Standby button to send the PC into standby mode.

✦ **Hibernate.** If standby is not enabled, the left button is labeled "Hibernate." Click this button to send the PC into hibernate mode. Press and hold the **SHIFT** key to change the Standby button to Hibernate.

✦ **Cancel.** Click this button to cancel the shutdown process and return to the desktop.

 In addition to turning off your computer, you can also log off by clicking the start menu and clicking the Log Off button, then clicking the Log Off button in the Log Off Windows dialog box. The logoff process closes your desktop and returns you to the logon screen. Logging off is especially useful if multiple people use your PC; doing so gives the next user quick access to the logon screen. Logging off also prevents others from easily accessing your personal data. You'll learn more about logging off in Chapter 6.

Hibernation and Standby

The Hibernate and Standby options are easily confused. Hibernation saves your desktop and system state to the hard drive, and then turns off the PC. The next time you power up your PC, you return to your desktop exactly as it was before. Hibernation returns you to your desktop more quickly than a normal startup, making it useful if you plan to be away from your PC for a long while or if you're not sure of a steady supply of power to the PC.

Standby, on the other hand, saves your desktop and system state to memory, and then puts the system into a low-power operating state without actually turning the PC off. The next time you press the power button or another key, you return to your desktop exactly as you left it. You can use standby mode if you need to leave your PC for a short period of time but want to be able to quickly return to your desktop, while reducing energy consumption at the same time while you are away.

 Although using standby returns you to your desktop more quickly than hibernation, it does expose your system to the possibility of data loss. If a PC loses power while on standby, even for a moment, all data stored in memory (that is, any data that has not been saved to the hard drive) will be lost.

Most notebook PCs support the standby feature, as does an increasing number of desktop PCs. Likewise, most PCs support Windows XP's hibernation feature.

Emergency Shutdown

Performing a proper shutdown is preferred over any other shutdown process—this allows the PC to save its data and turn itself off. That said, you might not always get the opportunity to perform a proper shutdown. If your system hangs, freezes, or otherwise becomes unresponsive, your options for a proper shutdown may be limited or non-existent.

In the event your system becomes frozen, the first thing you should do is press the **CTRL+SHIFT+ESC** key combination. This starts Windows Task Manager. In Windows Task Manager, click the **Shut Down** menu, and then select one of the shutdown options (Stand By, Hibernate, Turn Off, Restart, Log Off, or Switch User), as shown in Figure 3-4.

Figure 3-4 The Shut Down menu in Windows Task Manager.

If you are unable to open the Task Manager or access the Shut Down menu, wait about 10 minutes. In some cases, a frozen system returns to a functioning state if left alone for a while. As a last resort, press the power button on the system unit. You may have to hold the button in for several seconds before the power is cut off. After the power goes off, wait a few moments before turning the power back on to restart your PC. During the reboot after a manual power termination, the PC may perform additional checks to make sure the system is working properly.

A comparison of Windows XP's various shutdown options and when to use them appears in Table 3-1.

3

Table 3-1 When to use the various shutdown options.

ISSUE	TURN OFF	RESTART	HIBERNATE	STANDBY	EMERGENCY SHUTDOWN
End of day or finished working with PC	✔		✔		
New device drivers installed		✔			
New application installed		✔			
Save desktop, turn off power			✔		
Save desktop, maintain power			✔	✔	
Regain access to desktop as fast as possible				✔	
Regain access to desktop faster than a normal power up			✔	✔	
Save desktop, but notebook PC battery power is low				✔	
Electricity is about to go out	✔		✔		
Need to turn off PC quickly	✔		✔		
System not responding					✔

CHAPTER

Get Comfortable with Your Mouse and Keyboard

J ust as you use pedals and a steering wheel to control your car, you use your PC's mouse and keyboard to control your computer. While using a keyboard sounds easy enough, you can rest assured that the mouse is just as easy to use, since a computer mouse is very mild-mannered and harmless. With the mouse, you point to objects on your screen and issue commands. Using your keyboard, you enter text, numbers, and symbols, as well as manage other pieces of your PC's activity. Without a mouse and a keyboard, your computer would basically be useless.

This chapter explains these all-important devices and shows you how to use and control them so you can interact with your PC. You'll also take a quick look at how a notebook computer features a built-in mouse and keyboard combination and finally, you'll discover a fun way to practice using your mouse by playing a game of Solitaire, which is already installed on your computer.

Learning About Your Mouse

Most mouse devices have two buttons, the primary and secondary buttons, with a small wheel button nestled between them. By default, the primary button is the one on the left, and the secondary button is the one on the right.

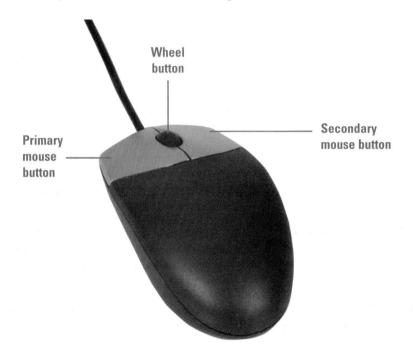

Wheel button

Secondary mouse button

Primary mouse button

Moving Your Mouse Pointer

Using your mouse involves two basic actions: moving the mouse to correctly position your mouse pointer (a small, white, left-pointing arrow that appears somewhere on your screen) over an object, button, menu, or other screen item; and clicking either the primary or secondary button on your mouse in order to perform some sort of action. Before you can move your mouse to position the mouse pointer, however, you should learn the proper hand placement for controlling your mouse device. Gently place your pointer finger on the primary mouse button and your middle finger on the secondary mouse button. Figure 4-1 shows the correct hand placement.

Figure 4-1 Proper hand placement for controlling the common mouse.

Once you've placed your hand on the mouse, simply slide the mouse across your mouse pad. The mouse pointer on the screen moves in the same direction as the mouse in your hand. If you hit the edge of your mouse pad or the extent of your reach, simply pick up the mouse, set it in the center of your mouse pad, and continue moving. As you become more experienced with the mouse, you'll find that you lift it often to reposition your hand for more comfortable operation.

For Lefties Only . . .

If you're left-handed, you may find that moving your mouse to the left-hand side of the keyboard is more comfortable. That way, you can use your left hand to maneuver the mouse. If you do, it's a good idea to reverse the mouse buttons, so that the right button becomes the primary button and the left button becomes the secondary button.

To change the orientation of the mouse from right-handed to left-handed, perform the following steps:

1 Click start, and then click Control Panel.

2 The Control Panel opens. Click Printers and Other Hardware.

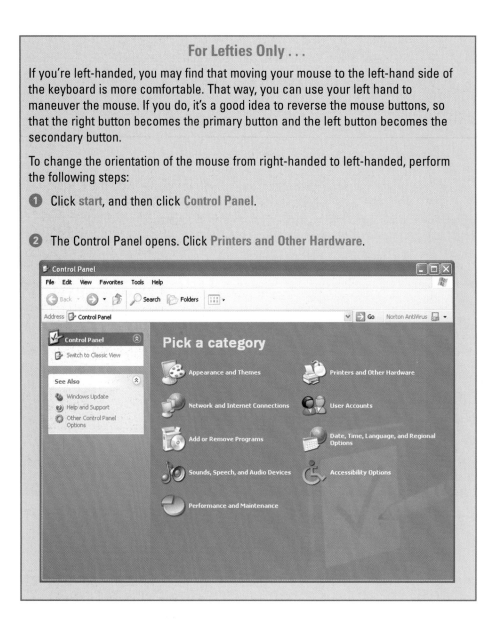

③ The Printers and Other Hardware screen appears. Click Mouse.

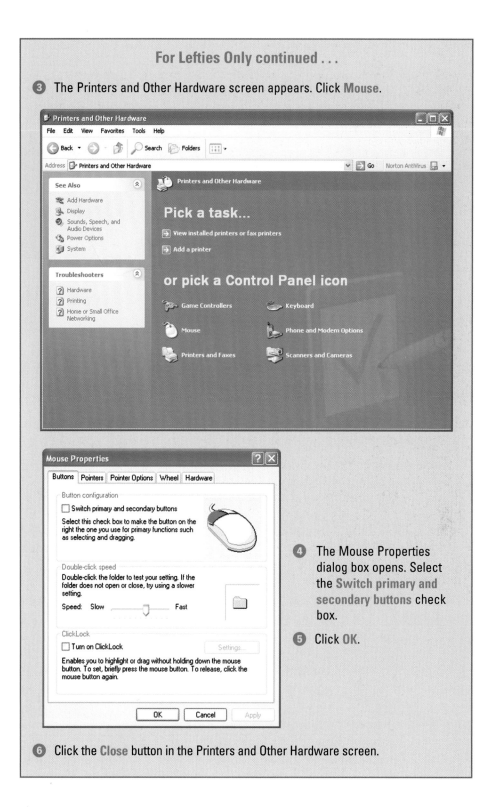

④ The Mouse Properties dialog box opens. Select the Switch primary and secondary buttons check box.

⑤ Click OK.

⑥ Click the Close button in the Printers and Other Hardware screen.

The shape of the mouse pointer may change depending on what type of screen element it's resting on or, if you've clicked one of the mouse buttons, what action you've instructed your PC to perform. As shown in the following table, you might see any of the following pointer images:

POINTER	DESCRIPTION
▷	An arrow is used to select objects.
I	An I-beam (shaped like a capital "I") is used when editing documents to place the pointer where the next letters will be inserted, modified, or deleted. This is called the insertion point.
↙ ✛	A thin arrow with two heads or a set of crosshairs indicates that an object can be moved or resized.
⧖	An hourglass indicates that some action is underway.
▷⧖	An arrow with an hourglass indicates that although the PC is busy performing some task, you can continue to select objects and initiate other tasks.
👆	A pointing finger indicates the presence of a hyperlink on an Internet document or Web page. You can click a hyperlink to open a file or go to another page.

More About . . . Pointer Images

If you're not thrilled with the pointer images Windows uses by default, you can change them by selecting a different pointer scheme. For example, one pointer scheme uses pointer images that look like dinosaurs! You select an alternative pointer scheme using Control Panel.

Clicking

The most common mouse action is the click. To click, you position the pointer over an object on your screen. Then, without twitching the mouse, press and release the primary mouse button. When you click an object, it becomes highlighted; this indicates that the object is selected.

To get the hang of clicking, try the following:

1 Move the mouse pointer so it rests over the **Recycle Bin** icon on your desktop. After a moment, a ToolTip appears, informing you that the Recycle Bin contains files and folders you have deleted.

> ### More About . . . ToolTips
>
> If you're not certain what a particular object on your screen does, try resting your mouse pointer on it for a second or two. A ToolTip may appear, providing basic information about the object.

2 Click once on the **Recycle Bin** icon. Notice that the icon itself and the name under the icon become highlighted, as shown in Figure 4-2. This indicates that the object is selected. Any action you instigate using the mouse or keyboard will affect the selected object.

Figure 4-2 The Recycle Bin icon after it has been clicked.

3 Click anywhere on the desktop, but not on the Recycle Bin icon or the taskbar. (The taskbar is the long bar at the bottom of your screen.) Notice that the Recycle Bin icon is no longer highlighted, indicating that it is no longer selected.

④ Click the **start** button. The start menu appears, as shown in Figure 4-3.

Figure 4-3 The start menu.

⑤ Click anywhere on the desktop, and the start menu disappears.

Double-Clicking

Some objects require you to double-click the primary mouse button in order to initiate an activity. This action is similar to clicking, except you click the button twice, quickly, without moving the mouse.

 Beginners often unintentionally twitch the mouse between clicks. This puts the pointer in a different place for each click, which the computer interprets as two single-clicks. If the mouse pointer moves on the screen before or while you click, you might perform some action or issue some command you didn't intend.

To practice double-clicking, try the following:

① Double-click the **Recycle Bin** icon on the desktop. The Recycle Bin window opens.
② Click the **Close** button (the X in the upper-right corner) in the Recycle Bin window. The Recycle Bin window closes.

Dragging

Dragging, also called clicking and dragging, is a technique that enables you to move text, graphics, files, and objects of any kind on your screen. Simply position your mouse pointer on the object to be moved, press and hold down the primary mouse button, and slide the mouse. Depending on what type of object you're dragging, either the object will move across the screen or the mouse pointer will change into an arrow with a box below it to indicate an object in motion. When the object reaches its destination, release the primary mouse button to place, or drop, the object in that location.

Dragging also enables you to resize windows, extend selections, and more.

Work through the following steps to practice dragging objects:

1. Position the mouse pointer over the **Recycle Bin** icon.
2. Press and hold down the primary mouse button.
3. Move the mouse. Notice that the Recycle Bin icon moves with the mouse pointer.
4. Position the **Recycle Bin** icon in the upper-right corner of the desktop, as shown in Figure 4-4.

Figure 4-4 Moving an object using click and drag.

⑤ Release the mouse button.

⑥ Repeat steps 1 through 5 to return the Recycle Bin icon to its original location.

 Use your ability to move objects with care. You can safely move any document or file you create, such as a word-processing document or a photo. You can even move objects around within a document, such as repositioning a picture in a greeting card. Moving system and software files from their original folders, however, can cause problems because the system may not know how to find them once they've been moved. As with real estate, location is crucial for these files!

 If you try to move a desktop icon and it does not move, the Auto Arrange feature is probably enabled. Auto Arrange automatically arranges all desktop icons in columns and rows starting at the upper-left corner of the screen. To disable this feature so you can move objects around the desktop, right-click over an empty area on the desktop. In the shortcut menu that appears, select **Arrange Icons By**, and then click **Auto Arrange**. If the Auto Arrange check box is selected, the feature was enabled. Clear the check box to disable the feature.

Selecting Objects

You know that you can select an object on your screen by clicking it. But what if you want to perform the same action on multiple objects, such as moving several icons from one part of your desktop to another? Rather than dragging each icon to the new location one-by-one, you can select all the icons you want to move and drag them to the destination, all at the same time.

To select multiple objects, place the mouse pointer near the set of objects you want to select. Then, press and hold down the primary mouse button and drag the mouse pointer across the objects to be selected. A shaded box appears, with one corner located where you first clicked the mouse button and the opposite corner located at your current mouse-pointer position. As you enclose objects within this box, they become highlighted, indicating that they have been selected (see Figure 4-5). When all the necessary objects are selected, release the primary mouse button, and perform the desired action using your mouse or keyboard.

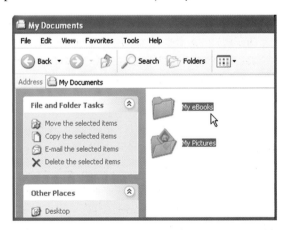

Figure 4-5 A click-and-drag selection action performed within Windows Explorer.

Let's practice selecting multiple objects:

1 Click **start**, and then click **My Computer**.

2 The My Computer window opens. Place your pointer to the left of the bottom row of icons.

3 Press and hold down the primary mouse button.

4 Move the mouse pointer toward the upper-left portion of the window. Notice how objects become selected as you drag the selection box over them, as shown in Figure 4-6.

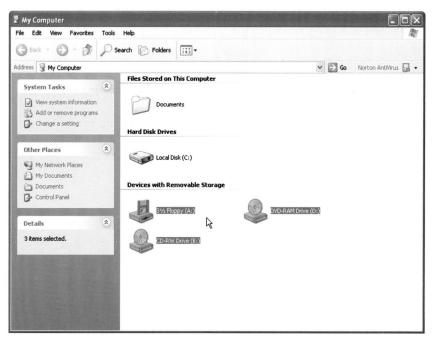

Figure 4-6 Selecting multiple objects with click and drag.

5 When you've selected a few of the objects, release the mouse button.

6 Once objects are selected, you can perform an action, such as opening, copying, or exploring all selected objects at once. At this time, however, refrain from performing any of these actions. Instead, close the My Computer window by clicking the **Close** button.

Right-Clicking

Although the secondary mouse button is used less frequently than the primary button, it has several interesting tricks up its sleeve. If you click the secondary button once (this is called right-clicking), a shortcut menu appears. A shortcut menu is a menu that is context or content sensitive; that is, the object or objects under the mouse pointer determine the commands that appear in the menu. You can also use the secondary mouse button to drag selected objects to a new location and then select a command from a shortcut menu.

To get a handle on right-clicking, do the following:

1 Right-click an empty area of the desktop.

2 A shortcut menu appears. Click the primary mouse button anywhere else on the desktop.

3 The menu disappears. Click **start**, and then click **My Computer**.

4 The My Computer window opens. Double-click **Local Disk C:**.

5 The contents of drive C: are displayed. Right-click any file and hold down the mouse button.

6 Drag your pointer to an empty area in the window and release the button.

7 A shortcut menu appears, as shown in Figure 4-7. Notice the commands that appear in the shortcut menu.

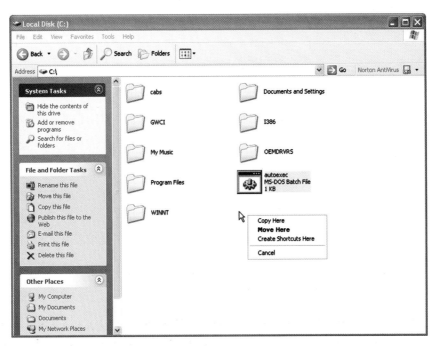

Figure 4-7 Shortcut menus appear when you right-click, drag, and drop.

8 At this time, do not select any of the commands. Instead, move your pointer to an empty area and click the primary mouse button. The shortcut menu closes, and action stops.

9 Click the **Close** button in the My Computer window to close it.

Using the Wheel Button

When a window isn't big enough to display the entire contents of a document or page, vertical and/or horizontal scroll bars appear (see Figure 4-8). These allow you to scroll up and down or left and right through the page or document so you can view all its contents. To use the scroll bars, you simply click on one of the arrows on either end of the scroll bar, or drag the scroll box (the small box that appears in the scroll bar) in the direction you want to scroll.

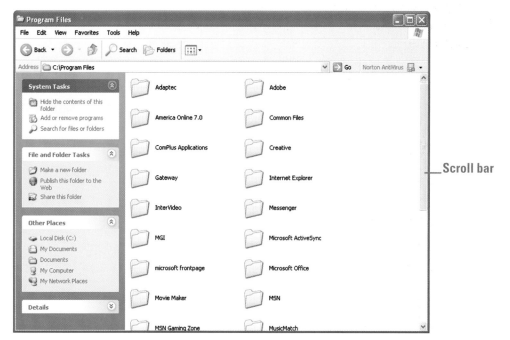

Scroll bar

Figure 4-8 A window with a scrollbar.

Alternatively, you can use the wheel button on your mouse to scroll through your document. This button is multi-functional—it can be either rotated or clicked. Typically, rotating the wheel allows you to scroll up and down through the text or graphics in a window to view all its contents. Pressing the wheel until it clicks, on the other hand, locks your mouse into scroll mode; in this mode, the mouse pointer changes to a two-headed arrow inside a circle, as shown in Figure 4-9. When in scroll mode, you can simply move your mouse to quickly scroll up and down in a window. (Click the wheel again to turn scroll mode off.)

Figure 4-9 The scroll-mode mouse pointer.

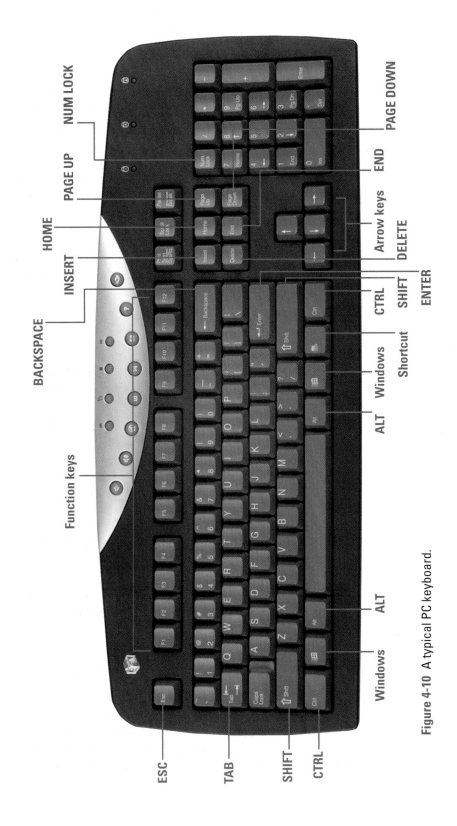

Figure 4-10 A typical PC keyboard.

Working with Your Keyboard

If you've ever used a typewriter, then your PC's keyboard should look somewhat familiar. As shown in Figure 4-10, computer keyboards, like typewriters, contain keys that enable you to input letters, numbers, and symbols. In fact, the layout of the letters, numbers, and symbols on your PC's keyboard mirrors that of typewriters of old.

You may notice, however, that your keyboard contains several keys not found on traditional typewriters. These additional keys, whose functions are described in Table 4-1, enable you to use your keyboard to issue commands and control many aspects of your PC's activity.

Table 4-1 Common keys and their uses.

KEY	USE
ALT and CTRL	The ALT and CTRL keys are sometimes used in combination with each other and the SHIFT key to send special commands to your PC.
SHIFT	Press the SHIFT key in combination with a letter key to enter uppercase letters.
Arrow keys	Press the arrow keys to move the insertion point within a document or move the selection highlight from one option or command to another within a menu or a dialog box.
Windows and Shortcut	Press the Windows key to open the start menu, or press the Shortcut key to open a shortcut menu based on the pointer's location.
ESC	Press the ESC key to exit the current menu, dialog box, or window. In some cases, it closes a program, but not always.
Function keys	The function keys are those keys marked F1, F2, and so on, through F12. The F1 key usually opens help information. Programs often assign special features or commands to function keys; to learn how a particular program uses these keys, read its documentation.
BACKSPACE	Press the BACKSPACE key to delete the character immediately to the left of the insertion point, to delete selected object(s), or to move backward in a wizard or dialog box.
ENTER	Press the ENTER key to start a new paragraph when working within a document. It can also be used to execute a selected command within a menu or dialog box.
INSERT	Press the INSERT key to toggle text-editing modes from overwrite to insert mode. The default setting is insert mode. In insert mode, keystrokes you type are added into a document, shifting the existing text to make room. In overwrite mode, for every key you press, a character to the right of the insertion point is deleted.

4

Key	Use
DELETE	Press the DELETE key to delete the character immediately to the right of the insertion point or to delete selected object(s).
HOME and END	Press the HOME key to move the insertion point to the beginning of the current line within a document, or CTRL+HOME to move the insertion point to the beginning of the document. Pressing the END key moves the insertion point to the end of the current line, while pressing CTRL+END moves the insertion point to the end of the document.
PAGE UP and PAGE DOWN	Press the PAGE UP and PAGE DOWN keys to scroll up or down within a document or window, one page at a time.
NUM LOCK	Many keyboards include a numeric keypad on the far right side; this keypad works like a standard accounting 10-key pad and is great for entering numeric data. To enable the numeric keypad and illuminate the Num Lock indicator light on the keyboard, press the NUM LOCK key. If the numeric keypad is already enabled, press the NUM LOCK key to disable it; when the keypad is disabled, you can use its keys as arrow keys as well as PAGE UP, PAGE DOWN, END, HOME, INSERT, and DELETE keys.

There are many other features and functions for a keyboard, which typically rely on multi-key combinations discussed throughout this book to enter commands. Make yourself familiar with the layout and the keys available on your keyboard to help you get the most out of your PC.

More About . . . Keyboards

Some PCs come equipped with multifunction keyboards. Multifunction keyboards provide additional capabilities. Such added capabilities take the form of additional keys or buttons that speed access to programs or places you visit or use most often. With a push of a button, you can jump to the Internet, open e-mail, play a CD, open the Help system, or launch a word processor. Some keyboards offer CD and DVD controls so you can play, pause, stop, skip forward or back, or adjust the volume while listening to music or watching your favorite movies. Often you can program extra buttons to perform customized tasks or activities. Some keyboards incorporate track balls or touch pads, so you won't even need a separate mouse.

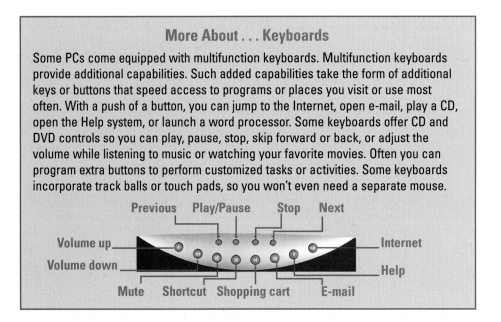

Using Your Notebook Mouse and Keyboard

Just as you use a mouse and keyboard to control and interact with your desktop computer, you use a mouse and keyboard to work with your notebook PC. Although your notebook PC's input devices operate in much the same way as your desktop computer's, there are a few minor differences.

Learning About Your Notebook Mouse

Many notebook PCs include a built-in mouse. Although the most common type of notebook mouse is a touchpad, shown in Figure 4-11, other systems might incorporate

 a trackball or a small joystick. In most notebook models, the mouse sits between the keyboard and the front edge of the notebook case and is accompanied by two mouse buttons that operate in the same way as the buttons on a more traditional mouse.

4

Figure 4-11 The touchpad on a Gateway® notebook PC.

To use a touchpad, lightly press one finger on the pad and slide it around. The mouse pointer on the screen tracks your finger's motion. Once you've positioned the pointer over an object or a command, you can perform all the same functions as with a regular mouse:

+ To click an object, either click the primary notebook mouse button or tap once on the touchpad.

+ To perform a double-click operation, simply double-tap the touchpad or double-click the primary notebook mouse button.

+ To drag, place the pointer on your starting point, click and hold the primary button, and then slide your finger to move the pointer to the desired destination.

+ To right-click, simply click the secondary notebook mouse button.

On a notebook PC that has a trackball or small joystick instead of a touchpad, you can apply these same principles. Rolling the ball or leaning the joystick moves the mouse, and pressing down on the ball or joystick is the same as pressing the primary mouse button.

If you find it challenging to use a notebook's built-in mouse, you can attach a traditional mouse to the notebook, as shown in Figure 4-12. Most notebooks have external peripheral ports on the back, front, and/or sides of their cases. You need only determine whether you have a serial, PS/2, or USB mouse, find a matching port on your notebook, and plug the mouse in. If you attach a serial or PS/2 mouse, you must restart the PC so it can detect the new mouse. If you attach a USB mouse, however, the system usually finds it automatically.

Figure 4-12 A notebook with a typical external mouse attached.

Understanding Your Notebook Keyboard

To save on space, notebook computers sometimes use keyboards with fewer keys than a traditional keyboard. To accommodate a smaller layout, some keyboards include only one SHIFT, ALT, CTRL, and Windows key instead of two. Other smaller keyboards keep these doubled keys, but turn some keys, such as PAGE UP, PAGE DOWN, HOME, END, NUM LOCK, and so on, into function options available only in combination with other keys. If so, you will see an FN or function key that you must use like a SHIFT key to access function-key commands.

Playing Solitaire

If you've played Solitaire in the past with a deck of cards, playing its computer counterpart is just as fun and addictive, with the added benefit of helping to improve your mouse skills. The computer version of Solitaire, shown in Figure 4-13, is exactly the same as its real-world counterpart, except that you use your mouse instead of your hands to move cards from one stack to another.

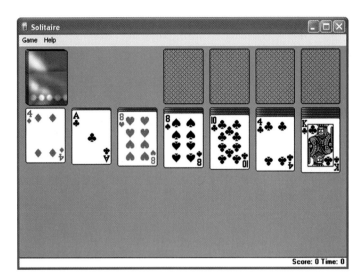

Figure 4-13 The Solitaire window.

If you've ever played Solitaire with a deck of cards, the screen looks very familiar to you. If you haven't, here is a brief introduction to the game. The deck is located in the upper-left corner of the Solitaire window. The object of the game is to use all the cards in the deck to build up the four suit stacks from ace to king in the upper-right portion of the window. To free up cards that you need to build the suit stacks, you build seven row stacks. For example, if you've uncovered the ace of hearts and moved it to the suit stack area, you must place the two of hearts on top of it, followed by the three of hearts, and so on. When you complete all four suit stacks, you win the game.

To become familiar with Solitaire, let's try it. Click the **start** button, point to **All Programs**, point to **Games**, and then click **Solitaire**. If you want some helpful tips on playing the game, review the following list.

+ Begin playing by double-clicking any aces on top of the seven row stacks to move them to the spaces at the top-right of the screen.

+ All cards in a suit stack must be of the same suit. Suit stacks begin with the suit's ace (ace is low) and ascend in numerical order to king.

- Check to see if there are any cards in the seven row stacks that can be added to a suit stack.

- Double-click a card to move it to a suit stack. (If you attempt an illegal move, Solitaire puts the card back.)

- Row stacks begin with the card Solitaire dealt and alternate between black and red in descending order. Any suit can be placed in any row stack.

- You can move a single card or the entire row from one row stack to another. To move a card or a stack of cards to another row, drag it.

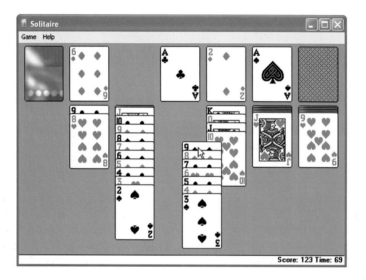

- The card moves with the pointer. When you release the button, the card stays where you put it.

- When you have made all the available plays on the board, click the deck to begin turning over cards. The card that is face up immediately to the right of the deck is always available for play.

- When a row stack becomes empty, you can replace it only with a king. Then you can begin building a new stack.

- You win the game when you move all cards from the deck into the suit stacks. You lose the game when you are unable to play any more cards.

✦ If you get stuck and can't find another move, declare the game lost and begin again. To start a new game, click the **Game** menu, and click the **Deal** command.

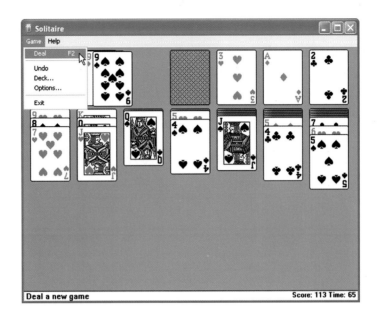

If you don't already know how to play a game, be it Solitaire or one of the other games included in Windows XP, you can access Help from within the game's program window. To access Help, click the **Help** menu, and then click **Contents**. This opens a window to access information on how to operate the game software. With what you already know about windows and dialog boxes, using Help should be much easier.

Not every game of Solitaire is winnable. If you find yourself going through the deck a few times without using any cards, double-check your rows. You may have overlooked a row-to-row move or a card that could be moved to a suit stack. You win the game if you use every card and complete the four suit stacks; you lose the game if you can't make another move.

More About . . . Games

The more you use your PC, the faster you become proficient at its use. Developing good mouse skills is important to getting the most out of your PC. A fun and easy way to develop these skills is by playing games. Windows XP includes FreeCell (a Solitaire-type game), Spider Solitaire, Hearts, Minesweeper, and Pinball. Open the Games submenu to easily access all of them. If your PC has Internet access, you can also play Internet Backgammon, Internet Checkers, Internet Hearts, Internet Reversi, and Internet Spades. So, play, play, play!

CHAPTER 5

Working with Windows XP and Its Programs

J ust like a car sitting idle in your driveway doesn't take you anywhere, a computer by itself does nothing. You have to have programs, sometimes referred to as applications, to perform tasks on the computer. Programs are designed to accomplish a specific type of function. For example, any time you play a computer game, write a letter, surf the Internet, or read your e-mail, you are using programs designed to execute the tasks.

One of the nice features of Windows is that all applications, in order to call themselves a Windows application, must follow certain guidelines. These guidelines provide a common interface between programs, which makes it much easier for you to work with different applications. The common tools include the various components of a window, wizards, and dialog boxes. To get the most out of your PC, you'll need to learn how to use these tools, as well as how to work with multiple programs simultaneously.

Discovering the Programs on Your PC

Windows XP is more than an operating system; it also includes several useful programs. Windows XP includes the following programs by default (see Figure 5-1).

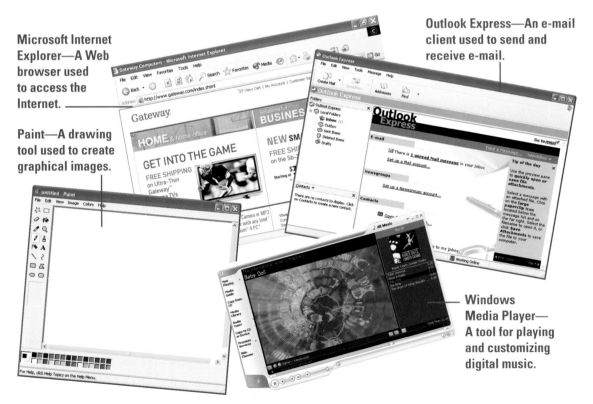

Microsoft Internet Explorer—A Web browser used to access the Internet.

Outlook Express—An e-mail client used to send and receive e-mail.

Paint—A drawing tool used to create graphical images.

Windows Media Player— A tool for playing and customizing digital music.

Figure 5-1 Windows XP includes loads of built-in programs of many kinds.

Your PC includes several pre-installed third-party programs. A third-party program is any program that is not included in the operating system. This includes programs by Microsoft as well as other software companies. Some examples of third-party programs you may find pre-installed on your system include games, anti-virus software, Microsoft Office (a suite of productivity software), photo-editing tools, system-management utilities, and custom configuration tools. And of course, you can always purchase and install additional programs you may need on your PC.

 This book introduces you to the basics of launching and interacting with Windows-based programs. It does not explore all of the various programs that came pre-installed on your computer. Fortunately, most software includes documentation, which you can read to get up to speed.

To determine which programs are installed on your computer, click the **start** button, point to **All Programs**, and browse the entries in this menu.

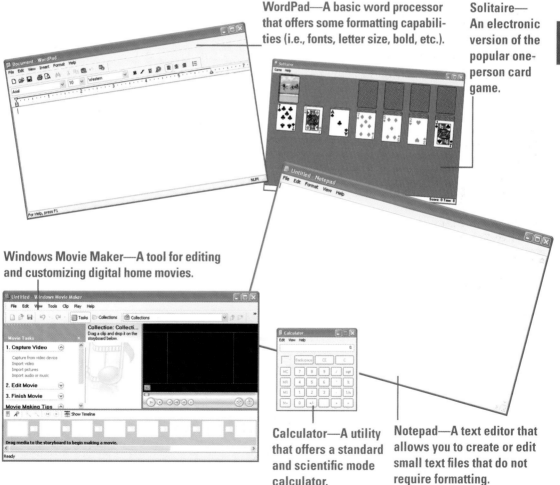

WordPad—A basic word processor that offers some formatting capabilities (i.e., fonts, letter size, bold, etc.).

Solitaire— An electronic version of the popular one-person card game.

Windows Movie Maker—A tool for editing and customizing digital home movies.

Calculator—A utility that offers a standard and scientific mode calculator.

Notepad—A text editor that allows you to create or edit small text files that do not require formatting.

Starting a Program

Before you can work with a program, you must first start it. To start a program, click its icon in the start menu. If the program is represented by an icon on the desktop, however, you can double-click the icon to start the program.

To get the hang of starting a program, let's start WordPad.

❶ Click the **start** button. The start menu appears.

❷ Position your mouse pointer over **All Programs** to view the first sublevel of the start menu.

❸ Position your mouse pointer over the **Accessories** folder. The Accessories sublevel of the start menu appears.

❹ Click **WordPad**. The WordPad program starts, and the WordPad window opens.

Now that WordPad is open, let's explore some common elements and controls of Windows programs.

Discovering a Window

Windows XP gets its name from its use of windows to display programs, files, information, and system settings. A window is a rectangular area displayed on your desktop that contains numerous common elements, such as a workspace, toolbars, a menu bar, and other standard controls. Almost every Windows-based program uses a window as its primary interface.

Figure 5-2 shows the window of a common Windows XP program, namely WordPad. As you can see, a thin, blue border defines the edges of the WordPad window, clearly separating it from the underlying desktop.

As shown in Figure 5-2, even the simplest window has many components.

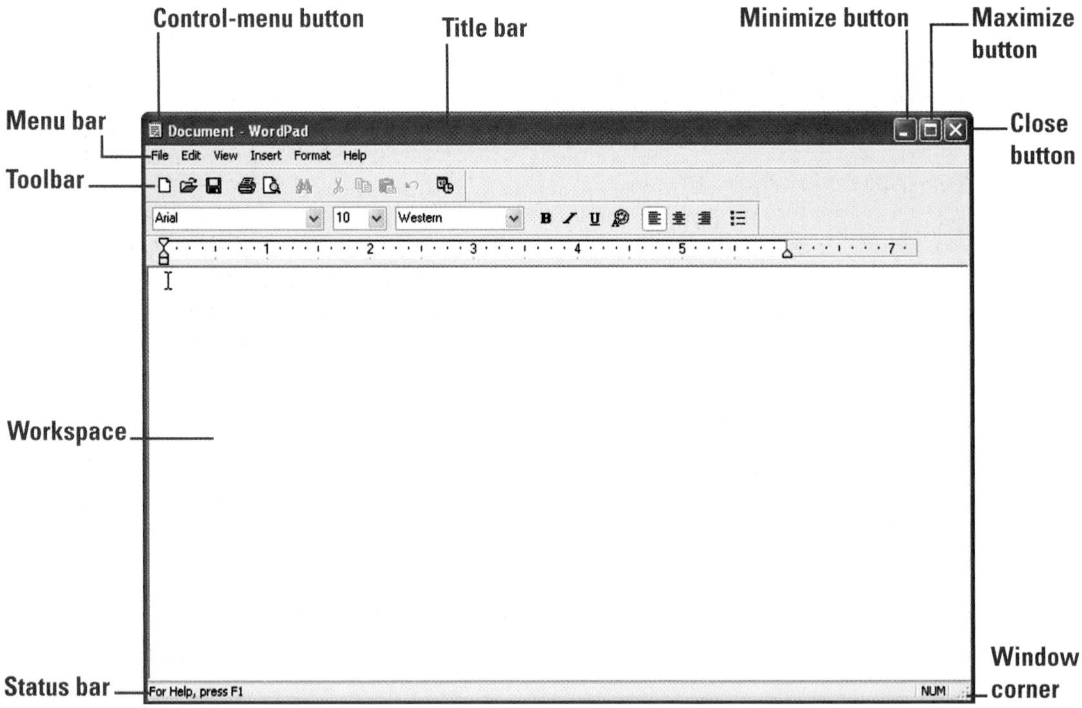

Figure 5-2 WordPad is a Windows-based program.

The Title Bar

Every window has a title bar, which displays the name of the program. When the window contains an open file, the title bar also displays that file's name. (The default name of new, unsaved documents is usually "Document.") In most cases, the name of the file appears first, and the name of the program appears second. The title bar shown in Figure 5-3 displays a file name of "Document" and the program name "WordPad."

▤ Document - WordPad   ⬓⬜✕

Figure 5-3 WordPad's title bar.

The title bar also includes the Minimize, Maximize/Restore Down, and Close buttons, as well as the control-menu button; all these are discussed in the sections that follow.

Moving Windows

Because Windows XP allows you to work with multiple windows, as discussed later in this chapter, at some point, you'll need to move an open window on your desktop. It could be to reveal the contents of another window or to access something on the desktop. To move a window, position the mouse pointer on the window's title bar, press and hold the mouse's primary button (avoid clicking title-bar buttons or the top edge of the window—you might issue some other command or perform a different action than intended), and drag the window to the desired location. When you release the mouse button, the window becomes set in its new position.

To practice moving a window, perform these steps:

❶ Position the mouse pointer on a window's title bar.

❷ Press and hold down the primary mouse button.

❸ Move the mouse around to move the window.

❹ Once the window is in the desired spot, release the mouse button.

5

The Minimize Button

Notice the three buttons on the right end of the title bar. The first of these buttons is the Minimize button. Click this button to minimize, or hide, the program window, thus

freeing up space on your desktop, without shutting down the program. When you minimize a window, the program remains open and running, but occupies no space on the desktop.

Minimize button

You might minimize a window in the following situations. You're finished working in a window for the time being, but may need to view it later. Instead of closing it, you can simply hide it. Or maybe you need to view the desktop or another window located behind the one that's currently open.

Notice that when a window is minimized, its taskbar button appears to be raised. To restore a minimized window to its previous size, simply click its taskbar button. Once the window is again displayed in the foreground, its taskbar button appears pushed in.

To learn how to use the Minimize button, work through the following steps:

1 If WordPad is not already running, start it. (Click the **start** button, point to **All Programs**, point to **Accessories**, and then click **WordPad**.) The WordPad window opens.

2 Click the **Minimize** button on the WordPad title bar. The WordPad window disappears, and the WordPad taskbar button appears raised.

3 Click the **WordPad** taskbar button. The WordPad window reappears, and the WordPad taskbar button appears pressed.

WordPad taskbar button

The Maximize/Restore Down Button

If the window covers only a portion of the desktop, you can maximize it to completely fill the screen. To maximize a window, click the Maximize button, located immediately to the right of the Minimize button.

Maximize button

Why maximize? You want the largest workspace possible—for example, if you are working on a long document and want to be able to see as much of it as possible at once. Or you want to hide other windows or the desktop itself.

 As a shortcut, double-click any blank area of the title bar to maximize its window.

When a window is maximized, the Restore Down button restores the maximized window to its original size.

Restore Down button

You might restore a window for various reasons. You may want to return a window to its original size. You can reduce the size of the window to view more than one window at a time. If you want to move a window, it needs to be restored. Maximized windows cannot be moved. See the "Moving Windows" sidebar that appeared earlier in this chapter.

Let's practice using the Maximize/Restore Down button.

❶ If WordPad is not already running, start it. (Click the **start** button, point to **All Programs**, point to **Accessories**, and then click **WordPad**.) The WordPad window opens.

❷ Click the **Maximize** button on the WordPad title bar. The WordPad window expands to fill the screen.

❸ Click the **Restore Down** button on the WordPad title bar. The WordPad window returns to its pre-maximized size.

The Close Button

Click the Close button, the button on the far right of the title bar, to close the program window and thus exit the program. If the program window contains a document that you have not yet saved, most programs will prompt you to save it before exiting.

Close button

You might need to close a window in numerous instances. For instance, you're finished using the window and want to exit the program, or the program is causing your system to run slower than normal.

Let's practice using the Close button. Do the following:

❶ If WordPad is not already running, start it. (Click the **start** button, point to **All Programs**, point to **Accessories**, and then click **WordPad**.) The WordPad window opens.

❷ Click the **Close** button on the WordPad title bar. The WordPad program stops running, the WordPad window closes, and the WordPad taskbar button disappears.

The Control-Menu Button

On the far-left side of the title bar is the control-menu button. As shown in Figure 5-4, you can click this button to open a menu of window commands, called the control menu.

 You can also access the control menu by right-clicking a program's taskbar button.

Figure 5-4 WordPad's control menu.

In most programs, the control menu contains six commands, as shown in Table 5-1.

 As with all Windows menus, commands that appear "dimmed" cannot be selected. For example, in Figure 5-4, the Restore command is dimmed because the window is not maximized. If the window were maximized, then the Restore command would be available, and the Maximize command would not.

Table 5-1 Control-menu commands.

COMMAND	DESCRIPTION
Restore	Selecting this command is the same as clicking the Restore Down button on the title bar.
Move	Select this command to move the current window around on the desktop. For more information about moving windows, refer to the section "The Title Bar" earlier in this chapter.
Size	Select this command to resize the window. You'll learn about resizing windows in the section "The Window Corner" later in this chapter.
Minimize	Selecting this command is the same as clicking the Minimize button on the taskbar.
Maximize	Selecting this command is the same as clicking the Maximize button on the taskbar when the window is not maximized.
Close	Selecting this command is the same as clicking the Close button on the taskbar.

The Menu Bar

Most windows include a menu bar, which appears just below the title bar. The menu bar contains a list of words or names, called menu names.

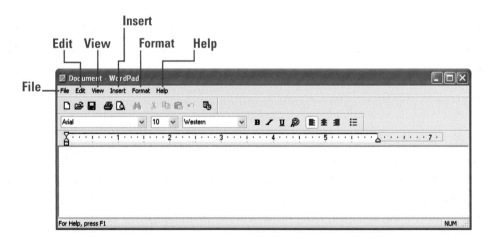

Click a menu name to reveal its program- or document-specific command menu (see Figure 5-5). Once the menu is open, move the mouse pointer to highlight the command you want; when the command is highlighted, click the primary mouse button to execute the command.

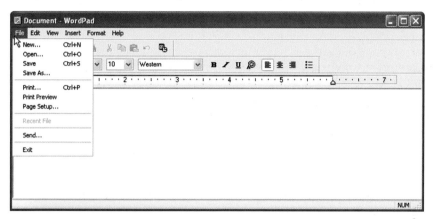

Figure 5-5 WordPad's File menu.

If you decide you don't want to execute a command, and instead want to close the open menu, do any of the following:

✦ Click the menu name a second time.

✦ Click anywhere in the program window or desktop outside of the menu area.

✦ Press the **ESC** key on your keyboard.

 If you click one menu name, but want to see the contents of another, reposition the mouse pointer over the second name. Doing so closes the first menu and opens the second.

Highlighting certain commands opens a submenu; when a submenu is present, an arrow appears beside the command. You select and execute submenu commands just as you do the commands on the main menus.

Toolbars

Many windows have toolbars, which appear below the menu bar but above the workspace. You click the buttons located on the toolbar to access common functions or perform common tasks. (In most windows, every toolbar button represents a command found in the menu bar.) Some toolbar buttons have commands or selections hidden within a drop-down list. Click the down arrow that appears right beside the toolbar button to access this list.

Toolbar buttons usually include a picture that represents the button's associated command. Even so, it is sometimes difficult to determine a button's function just by looking at it. To find out what command or function is associated with a particular button, position your mouse pointer over that button. After a moment, a ToolTip appears, explaining the button's function.

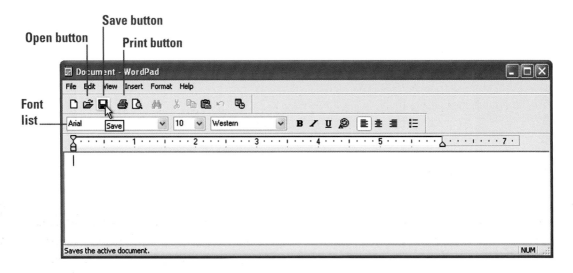

In addition to toolbar buttons, many toolbars feature drop-down combo boxes. For example, WordPad's toolbar contains drop-down combo boxes that enable you to set the font and point size of text in the WordPad document. To use a drop-down combo box, you can either type your selection in the text box or click the down-arrow to the right of the text box and click one of the options that appears. (You'll learn more about drop-down combo boxes in the section "Understanding Dialog Boxes" later in this chapter.)

Some drop-down combo boxes contain lists that are so long they contain a scroll bar. Drag the scroll box up and down the scroll bar to locate the option you want.

The Status Bar

Many windows feature a status bar, typically located along the window's bottom edge. The status bar displays window-specific information and messages. In WordPad, for example, the status bar displays the messages "For Help, press F1" and "NUM," as shown in Figure 5-6. (The first message indicates how you can receive help with the program, and the second indicates that the NUM LOCK key is toggled on.) The status bar in Windows Explorer, on the other hand, displays details about selected items. For example, when a drive is selected, the status bar displays its total free space; when a file is selected, the status bar displays details such as the file's type and size and the date it was last modified.

For Help, press F1 | NUM

Figure 5-6 WordPad's status bar.

 In some programs, the status bar displays information about a toolbar button when you position your mouse pointer over the button.

The Workspace

The workspace is the area between the toolbars and the status bar. In many windows, the workspace acts like a piece of paper. For example, in WordPad, the workspace is where the words you type appear. Likewise, in Paint, the workspace is where you "draw" and interact with your designs. In other programs, however, the workspace acts more like an interface. That is, you interact with the workspace by clicking buttons, choosing options from drop-down lists, and so on to complete a task. For example, the workspace in Calculator consists of the series of buttons you click to enter equations into the text box.

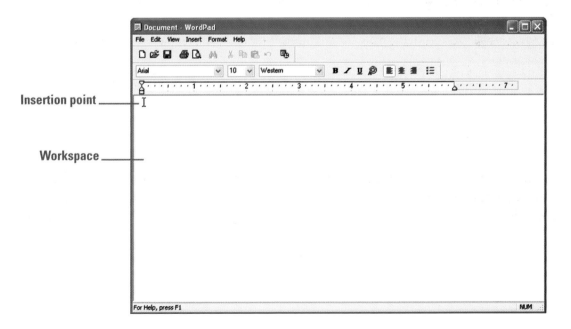

The Window Corner

As you work with windows, you may encounter instances when you need your window to be larger or smaller. Of course, one way to resize your window is to click the Restore Down button in the title bar (refer to the section "The Maximize/Restore Down Button" earlier in this chapter). Alternatively, however, you can use the window corner for more precise control. Located in the lower-right corner of the program window, the window corner enables you to alter both the height and the width of the window at the same time.

To resize a window using the window corner, perform the following steps:

1 Position your mouse pointer over the window corner, making sure the tip of the pointer is just inside the window border. The mouse pointer changes to a diagonal two-headed arrow.

The Sizing handle

2 Press and hold down the primary mouse button.

3 Drag your mouse slowly in any direction. Notice how the window size changes based on how you move the mouse.

4 Move the mouse so that the window is larger than it was before you started this exercise.

5 Release the mouse button.

6 Repeat steps 1 through 5, but this time move the mouse so that the window is smaller than it was before you started.

7 Release the mouse button.

All four corners of a window function just like the window corner. Simply position your mouse pointer over any corner, making sure the tip of the pointer is just inside the window border; the mouse pointer changes to a diagonal two-headed arrow. Then click and drag the mouse to resize the window.

 If you wish to resize the width but not the height of your window, position your mouse pointer on either side of the window border, click, and drag. Likewise, to resize the height only, place the pointer on the top or bottom window border, click, and drag.

Understanding Dialog Boxes

A dialog box is another item you'll frequently encounter. Dialog boxes appear when Windows XP needs more information to perform an operation or when it wants to confirm an operation. They often appear as a result of selecting certain menu commands. Dialog boxes let you tell the computer what you want it to do.

Although you may encounter any number of different dialog boxes while using your PC, all dialog boxes utilize pieces of a basic set of elements to gather information from you. For example, many dialog boxes use tabs (see Figure 5-7). A dialog box with tabs operates

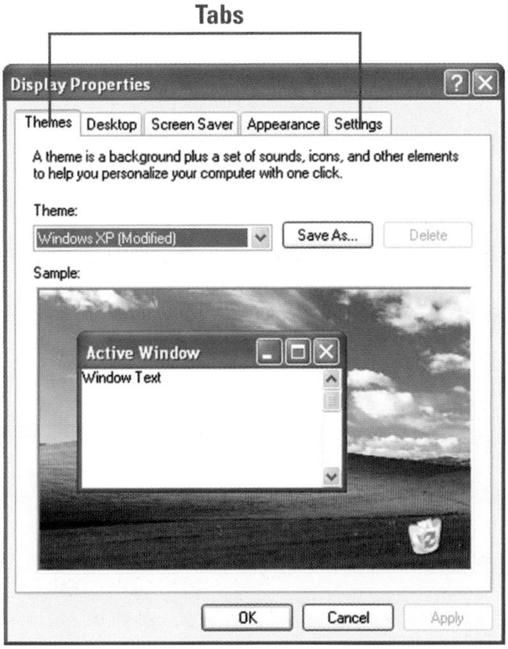

Tabs

Figure 5-7 A dialog box with tabs.

like a dictionary with tabs; you select a tab to display its contents, just as you turn to a tabbed page in a dictionary to view words that begin with the letter on the tab. Some dialog boxes only use a single tab, whereas others may have many. Some dialog boxes, on the other hand, don't use tabs at all (see Figure 5-8).

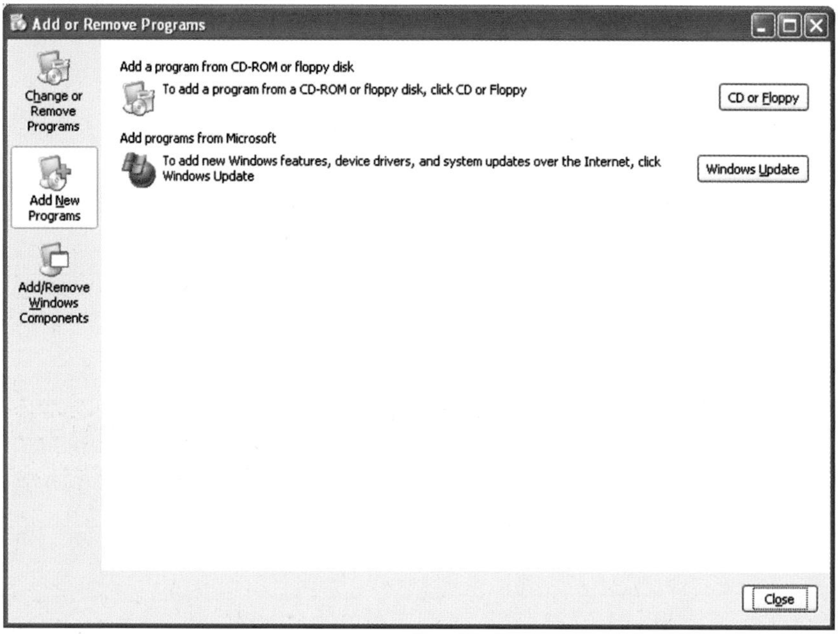

Figure 5-8 A dialog box without tabs.

Other elements commonly found in dialog boxes include:

◆ **Option buttons.** You use option buttons to select only one item from a list of options. If you attempt to select a second option button, the one selected first becomes deselected. To select an option button, simply click it; when an option button is selected, a dot appears inside it.

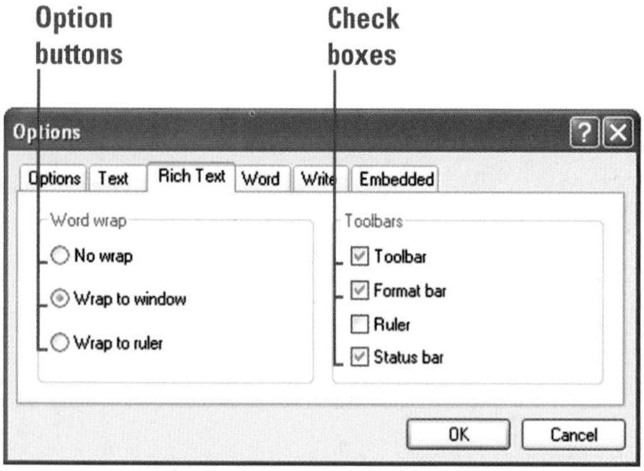

◆ **Check boxes.** Check boxes are used in lists of options in which more than one option can be selected, or when a single option can be turned on or off. To select a check box, click it; when a check box is selected, a small check mark appears inside it. To deselect a check box, simply click it to remove the check mark.

✦ **Object-selection fields.** An object-selection field is an area that lists one or more options. In most cases, you can select only a single item at a time; the selected item is highlighted.

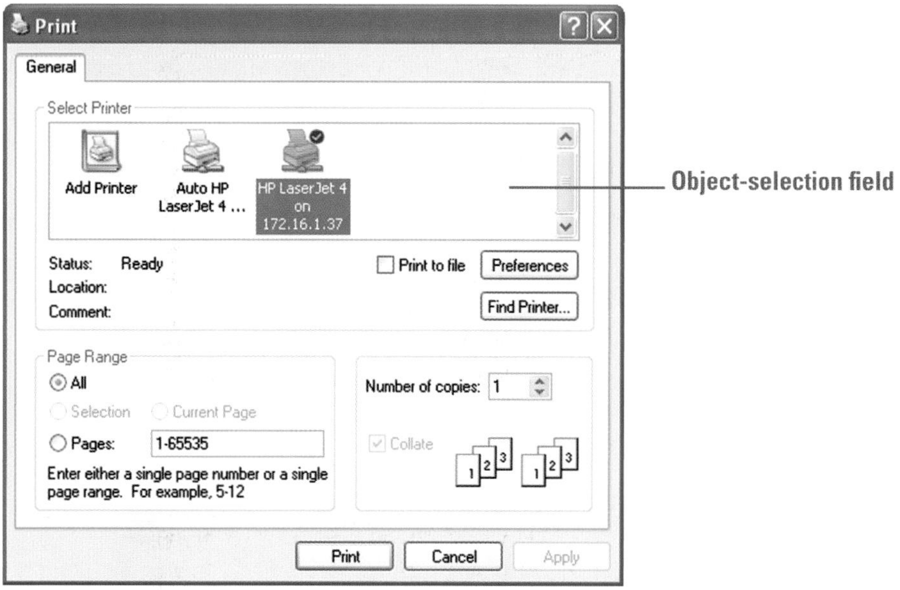

Object-selection field

✦ **List boxes.** List boxes contain a list of options from which the user can select. Some list boxes contain lists that are so long they contain a scroll bar; drag the scroll box up and down the scroll bar to locate the option you want.

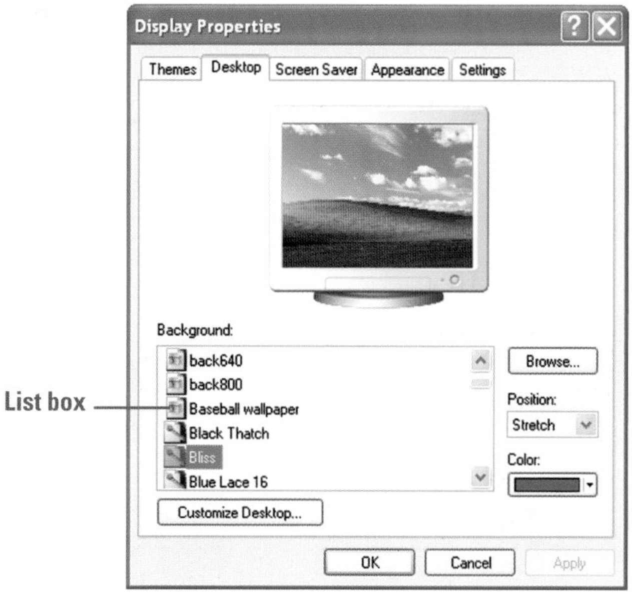

List box

✦ **Drop-down list boxes.** Drop-down list boxes work in the same way as regular list boxes, in that they contain a list of options from which the user can select. In order to view the list of options in a drop-down list, however, you must first click the drop-down arrow button that accompanies it. Some drop-down list boxes contain lists that are so long they contain a scroll bar; drag the scroll box up and down the scroll bar to locate the option you want.

✦ **Text boxes.** A text box is a box in which you can enter data, such as a file name or a range of pages, using your keyboard. In some instances, an option button or a check box accompanies text boxes. In such cases, the text box is available for use only if the option button or check box is selected.

Text box

Combo box

+ **Combo boxes.** These
  elements enable you to
  either type your selection
  in the text box or select it
  from the accompanying
  list box (hence the name
  combo box).

5

+ **Drop-down combo boxes.** With a drop-down combo box, you can either
  type your selection in the text box or select it from the accompanying drop-
  down list box.

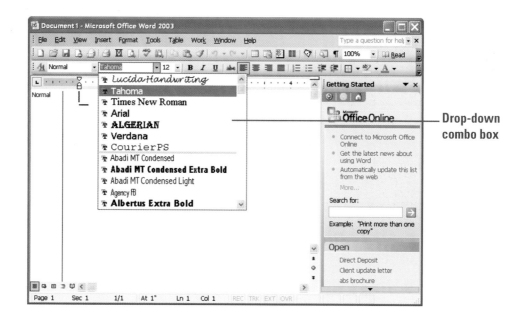

Drop-down
combo box

- **Spin boxes.** You use a spin box to input a numerical value. For example, in WordPad's Print dialog box, you use a spin box to specify how many copies of your document should be printed. To use a spin box, click the up- or down-arrow button to increase or decrease the displayed number by 1. Alternatively, instead of using the spin box's arrow buttons, you can simply type the desired number in the spin box's field.

- **Buttons.** Buttons are common in dialog boxes. You click them to execute a command or apply whatever settings you've selected in the dialog box. Common buttons include Close, Cancel, Apply, Print, Open, and Save; in most cases, the name or description on the button defines what that button does.

Using Wizards

A wizard is similar to a dialog box, in that it presents you with a series of options from which you must choose. But unlike a dialog box, which presents you with all the available controls, options, and selections at once or on multiple tabbed screens, a wizard presents them to you one at a time, in a specific order.

Wizards appear most often—and not by magic—when you initiate a system-configuration change or some other complex activity. In fact, you've already encountered a wizard if you worked through the manual printer installation process discussed in Chapter 3.

You navigate a wizard using the three buttons located at the bottom of the wizard screen:

✦ **Back.** The Back button isn't always present, but when it is, you can click it to return to the previous wizard screen in order to change your selections or settings.

✦ **Next.** Clicking the Next button advances the wizard to the next screen. In most cases, you must make a selection on the current wizard screen in order to activate the Next button.

✦ **Cancel.** Clicking Cancel stops the wizard and returns you to the previously active program or dialog box.

Add Printer Wizard

Specify a Printer
If you don't know the name or address of the printer, you can search for a printer that meets your needs.

What printer do you want to connect to?

◉ Browse for a printer

○ Connect to this printer (or to browse for a printer, select this option and click Next):

Name: [   ]

Example: \\server\printer

○ Connect to a printer on the Internet or on a home or office network:

URL: [   ]

Example: http://server/printers/myprinter/.printer

[< Back] [Next >] [Cancel]

Buttons on a wizard screen

Creating and Saving Files

Your computer most likely arrived with several programs installed—that is, software designed to create specific types of files or accomplish specific tasks. Likewise, programs include various commands and ways to save the documents or data files they use. Saving a document or file permits you to store it on your hard disk so you can access it again at another time.

Working with WordPad

WordPad is a word processing application included with Windows. You can use WordPad to write letters, notes, recipes, newspaper articles, or even books, all of which are referred to in Windows as documents. WordPad is great for simple documents.

To start WordPad, click the **start** button, point to **All Programs**, point to **Accessories**, and then click **WordPad**. The WordPad program window, shown in Figure 5-9, appears.

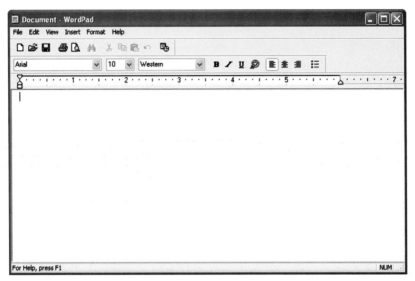

Figure 5-9 The WordPad program window.

Entering Text

The most basic action you can take within WordPad is to enter text. Every keystroke you perform on the keyboard appears in WordPad's workspace area. As you type, the blinking insertion point moves to the right to indicate where the next letter will be placed.

To practice entering text, do the following:

1 Type your name. Your name should appear in the workspace.

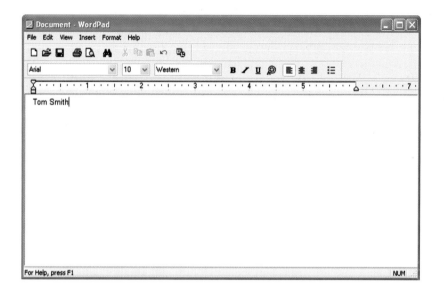

2 Press **ENTER**. The insertion point moves to the beginning of the next line.

3 Type your address, and then press **ENTER**.

4 Type your city, state, and ZIP, and then press **ENTER**.

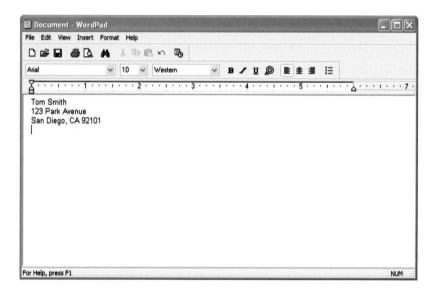

Inserting Text

The ability to insert text at any point in a document is one of WordPad's best features. For example, if you already typed your name and address, but decide you want to add your title before your name, you can simply insert it, as follows:

1 Move the pointer to the beginning of the first line, just before the first letter of the first word. Notice that the pointer is shaped like a capital "I" and is called an I-beam.

2 Click your primary mouse button. The blinking insertion point now appears before the first letter of the first word.

3 Type a title, such as Mr., Mrs., or Ms. The text appears before your first name.

4 After typing the title, press the **SPACEBAR** once to insert a space between the title and your first name.

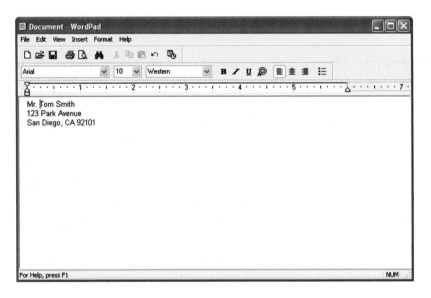

 You can position the insertion point anywhere within the existing document to add new text.

Deleting Text

Deleting text is just as easy as inserting it. In fact, WordPad offers several ways to delete text. One way is to use the BACKSPACE key:

1 Position the blinking insertion point between the space after the title and before your first name.

2 Press the **BACKSPACE** key once. The space is removed.

❸ Press the **BACKSPACE** key several more times until the title is completely removed.

The second method for deleting text is to use the **DELETE** key. First, repeat the steps to insert the title, and then follow these steps:

❶ Position the blinking insertion point before the first letter of the title.

❷ Press the **DELETE** key once. The first letter of the title is removed.

❸ Press the **DELETE** key several more times until the title is completely removed.

The third method is to use your mouse to select a section of text, be it a single character or multiple paragraphs, and then delete the entire selected text at once by pressing either the **BACKSPACE** key or the **DELETE** key. To do this, perform the following:

❶ Position the blinking insertion point immediately to the right of your last name.

❷ Press and hold down the primary mouse button, and drag the mouse pointer to the beginning of your first name. Your entire name should be selected.

❸ Press either the **BACKSPACE** key or the **DELETE** key once. The selected text vanishes.

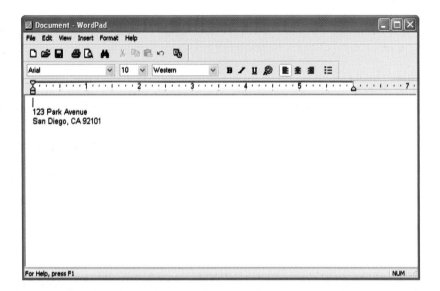

Undoing an Action

If you realize you've made a mistake and want to restore text that you deleted, you can either re-type it or use the Undo command in the Edit menu. This command reverses the last action taken within WordPad, such as a deletion, insertion, or text-formatting change. To practice using this command, click the **Edit** menu and click the **Undo** command. You can also click the **Undo** button on the toolbar. If you deleted your name in the preceding section, it is restored to your document in its original location.

 As an alternative to using the menu or toolbar, press the **CTRL+Z** key combination to issue the Undo command.

Replacing Text

When you replace text, you are deleting selected text and replacing it with new text that you type—in effect, deleting and inserting text at the same time. To replace text, follow these steps:

1 Position the blinking insertion point to the right of your last name.

2 Press and hold down the primary mouse button, and drag the mouse pointer to the beginning of your first name. Your entire name should be highlighted.

3 Type another name. The selected text is removed, and the new name is inserted in its place.

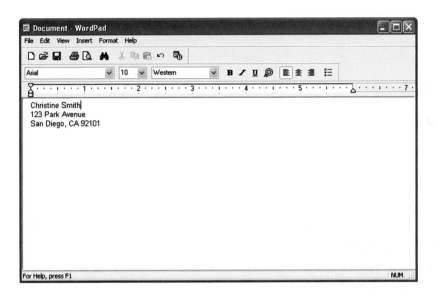

Understanding Wordwrap

As you type in the WordPad workspace, the text automatically flows from the end of one line to the beginning of the next. This automatic flow is known as wordwrap. Not only does WordPad wrap as you type, it is also smart enough to move an entire word from the end of one line to the beginning of the next one.

The only time you should press the **ENTER** key on your keyboard while working with WordPad is when you want to begin a new paragraph or force a new line. When you typed your address earlier, for example, each line ended when you pressed **ENTER**. In effect, you created three paragraphs.

To see wordwrap in action, you must type enough text to span the entire width of the workspace. Try the following:

① Position your blinking insertion point on a new line.

② Type a short note. When you reach the end of the line, the blinking insertion point automatically moves to the next line.

Document - WordPad

File   Edit   View   Insert   Format   Help

[Arial]   [10]   [Western]   **B** *I* <u>U</u>   ≣ ≡ ≡   ≔

```
Christine Smith
123 Park Avenue
San Diego, CA 92101

Dear Christine,

Your dad and I certainly hope you are enjoying your dorm room and your new life at college. We look forward to visiting
you soon. If you get a chance, please check out information on the local hotels.

Love,
Mom
```

For Help, press F1   NUM

Saving Your File

Until you save your document, it exists only in your PC's temporary memory. If you shut down the computer or otherwise lose power, that document will be lost. The only way to protect your document is to save it. This file can be stored on any storage device you can access, including hard drives, floppy drives, Zip drives, or a network drive. You should make a habit of saving every document you create. You might want to open a file, such as a recipe, grocery list, or letter to your aunt, at a later date to change or edit the information.

You don't have to wait until you've finished your document to save it. You can save early (perhaps even before you've typed any text in the document) and save often (every five or 10 minutes). That way, you won't lose any of your precious data!

The only difficult part about saving a document is deciding where on your system you want it to be stored. Think of your PC like a filing cabinet, in which each drawer represents a drive—one is your hard drive, another a floppy drive, and so on. Within each drawer, you can place pieces of paper. These are like files stored on a drive. You can also put manila folders in a drawer; these are like folders on a drive. A manila folder can hold pieces of paper (that is, files) or other manila folders (that is, folders).

 See Chapter 7 for more information about organizing your saved files into folders and subfolders.

When you attempt to save a file, Windows XP guides you to an automatic or default storage location, called My Documents, a folder on the hard drive that's part of your user profile. This is usually a fine place to store your documents. In fact, if you always use the same location, you'll always be able to find your documents in one place.

You specify where your document is saved in Windows XP's Save As dialog box. This dialog box, shown in Figure 5-10, contains many unique features.

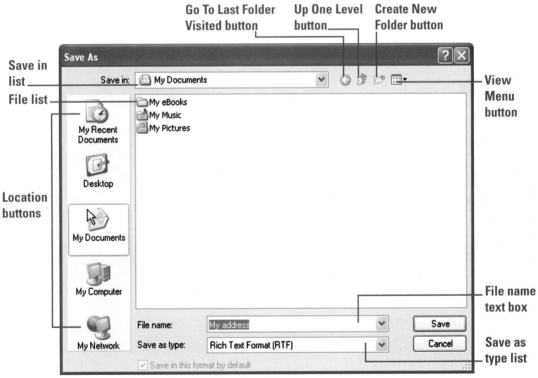

Figure 5-10 The Windows XP Save As dialog box.

Location buttons. Click a location button to quickly specify that the document you're saving be stored in that location. When you click a button, the location is displayed in the Look in list, and the file list displays the contents of the selected location.

Save in list. This drop-down list enables you to access the same locations as the five location buttons, as well as all local drives (floppies, hard drives, etc.) and the Shared Documents folder.

 Every storage device is known as a drive and has an associated drive letter. The primary hard drive on your PC is drive C:.

File list. The file list displays all the drives, folders, and files in the location you select. You can double-click a drive or folder icon to open that drive or folder and display its contents in the file list.

 As you open drives and folders, the Save in list is updated to reflect the current location.

Go To Last Folder Visited button. Click this button to return to the last location you selected.

Up One Level button. Click this button to navigate up the storage hierarchy of your system—that is, to move up one level in the Look in list in order to view the parent folder or drive of the currently selected folder. For example, if you are looking at the My Music folder, clicking Up One Level would change the context to the My Documents folder.

Create New Folder button. Click this button to create a subfolder within the current location. The new folder is displayed in the file list with the default name "New Folder."

 You can type a new name to replace "New Folder" with something more descriptive. To do so, simply type the new name in the text box. If you're performing this action long after creating the new folder and the file name is no longer highlighted, right-click the new folder and choose **Rename** from the shortcut menu that appears. This displays a text box around the folder's name; simply type a new name.

View Menu button. Click this button to display a menu of options that enable you to change how contents in the file list are displayed. Experiment with the different views until you find one that suits you.

File name text box. Type a name for the document you're saving in this text box. For example, in the following exercise in step 2 you define a filename for a document, such as My Address.

Save as type list. When you save a document, WordPad creates a file whose name ends with the three-letter file extension, .rtf. This file extension indicates that the file is of the type "RTF," short for "Rich Text Format." You can change a document's file type by selecting a different type from this drop-down list, but doing so is not advised unless you really know what you're doing.

More About . . . File Types

RTF is a file type, just as music files, video files, and image files are different file types. RTF files include not just the text you type into a document but also its formatting and layout. Other programs, such as Notepad and Microsoft Word, use different file types—namely, TXT and DOC respectively. "TXT" stands for text file, and it includes only plain text and spaces with no formatting. "DOC" stands for document and includes even more formatting and layout information than RTF.

Save button. Click this button to create a new file in the specified location with the specified name. The document is stored in that file.

When saving files, here are a few tips to keep in mind:

✦ The file name must be fewer than 255 characters long.

✦ Use any character on the keyboard, except for the following: / \ : * ? " < > |

✦ You should assign your files descriptive names so you can remember what they are without having to open them.

✦ You don't have to use My Documents to store your files, but being consistent and using the same location all the time is a good idea. You can always create subfolders within My Documents to organize your files.

To save the current document in WordPad, follow these steps:

❶ Click the **Save** button. The Save As dialog box appears. Notice that the location button for My Documents is selected, and that the Save in list selection has My Documents displayed.

You could also click the **File** menu, and then click the **Save As** command.

Save button

❷ In the File name text field, type a name for your document, such as My address.

❸ Click **Save**.

Your document is now stored as a file on your hard drive in the My Documents folder.

Once you've saved your document, close WordPad by clicking the **Close** button in the upper-right corner of the program window.

More About . . . Save and Save As

You should resave your file every ten minutes or so. To resave your file, keeping the same file name and file location, click the **Save** button on the WordPad toolbar or click the **File menu** and choose **Save**. WordPad will update the file with the changes—no questions asked.

If you want to save your file with a different file name or in a different location, click the **File menu** and select **Save As**. Using Save As opens the Save As dialog box, which allows you to enter a file name or location. Both the original saved file and the new Save As file will remain on your disk drive.

Opening A File

Now that you have a file stored on your hard drive, you can learn how to open a file. To open a file, follow these steps:

❶ Start **WordPad** from the start menu.

❷ Click the **Open** button on the toolbar; it's the one with an open folder on it. The Open dialog box opens; this dialog box is quite similar to the Save As dialog box. Notice that the location button for My Documents is selected, and that the Look in list has My Documents displayed.

 You could also click the **File** menu, and then click the **Open** command.

3 Click to select the document you saved previously.

 If your document was not saved in My Documents, use the navigational controls in the Open dialog box to locate the document file. These controls act just like their counterparts in the Save As dialog box.

4 Click **Open**. The document appears in the WordPad workspace.

Working with Multiple Programs

Windows XP enables you to run more than one program at a time, a feature you'll appreciate as you become more familiar with your PC and its various programs. For example, suppose you're typing a letter in WordPad and need some information from the Internet. With WordPad still open, you can quickly open Internet Explorer and find what you need. Or maybe someone sent you an e-mail message with information about a topic discussed in your letter. Again, with WordPad still open, you can start Outlook Express and find the message. Once you've found the information you want, you can switch back to WordPad and continue your letter where you left off.

 Windows XP can handle a large number of open programs at the same time, but just how many depends on how much memory your PC has. The more memory your PC has, the more programs you can run simultaneously.

Starting Multiple Programs

Whether your desktop is empty or already contains an open program window, you open a new program using the start menu or by double-clicking the program's desktop icon (if available). You do this to start the first program you want to open, the second program, the third program, and so on. To open several programs, do the following:

1 Click the **start** button, and then click **Control Panel**. The Control Panel window opens.

2 Click the **start** button, point to **All Programs**, point to **Accessories**, and then click **WordPad**. The WordPad window opens.

3 Click the **start** button, point to **All Programs**, point to **Accessories**, and then click **Paint**. The Paint window opens.

4 Click the **start** button, point to **All Programs**, point to **Games**, and then click **Solitaire**. The Solitaire window opens.

5 Click the **start** button, point to **All Programs**, point to **Accessories**, and then click **Calculator**. The Calculator window opens. Figure 5-11 shows the Windows XP desktop with all these programs open.

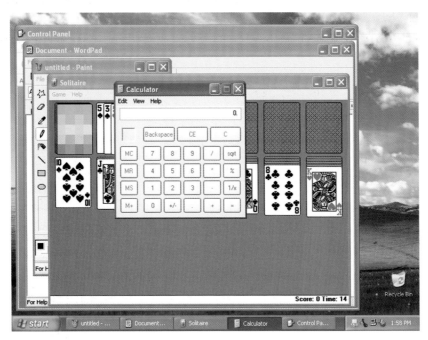

Figure 5-11 The Windows XP desktop with several windows open.

Switching Between Multiple Programs

When you have multiple programs running on your desktop, the ability to switch from one to another is crucial. With Windows XP, you can do this using a few different techniques:

✦ By clicking the desired program's window

✦ By clicking the desired program window's taskbar button

✦ By pressing the **ALT+TAB** keyboard shortcut

 In Windows XP, the active program is the one whose window has a darker title bar; the title bars of inactive program windows are more subdued in color. In addition, the active program's taskbar button appears pressed in, while taskbar buttons of inactive programs appear raised.

Clicking the Program's Window

To switch to another program, you can simply click anywhere in the desired program's window. To switch programs using this method, do the following (these steps assume your desktop looks like the one shown in Figure 5-11):

 Click any part of the **Solitaire** window. The Solitaire window becomes active and appears in front of all other windows.

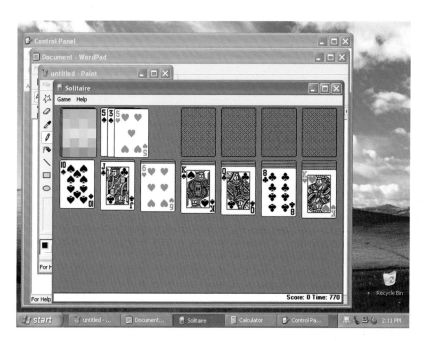

❷ Click any part of the **Paint** window. The Paint window returns to the front.

Clicking the Program's Taskbar Button

If the program window you want to activate is completely obscured by other open windows on your desktop, thus preventing you from clicking it, you can click the program's taskbar button instead. A program's taskbar button includes the program's icon, followed by a file or document name, followed by the program name. If a program doesn't use files or documents, or if neither is open, only the program name appears.

To practice switching programs using taskbar buttons, do the following (again, these steps assume your desktop looks like the one shown in Figure 5-11):

1 Click the **WordPad** taskbar button. The WordPad window becomes active and appears in front of all other windows.

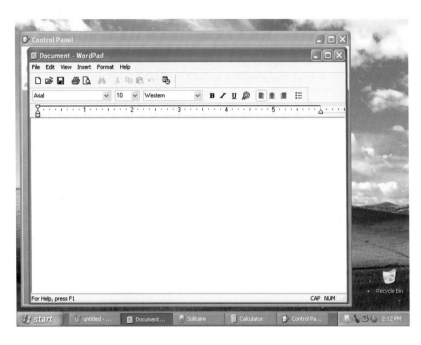

2 Click the **Paint** taskbar button. The Paint window returns to the front.

> ### More About . . . Taskbar Buttons
>
> There is no limit to the number of buttons the taskbar can hold. When numerous buttons are on display, however, they may be reduced in size (depending on your screen resolution) in order to fit on the taskbar. This usually means that less of the file and program name fits on the button. To view the entire file and program name for a taskbar button, position your mouse pointer over the button. After a few moments, a ToolTip appears, displaying whatever file- and program-name data is available.

If you have two or more windows open in a single program, and the taskbar holds six or more taskbar buttons, the taskbar collapses same-program windows into a single taskbar button, called a multi-window taskbar button. These types of buttons are indicated by the presence of a number between the icon and the program name. (This number also indicates how many windows are accessible from that button.) Multi-window taskbar buttons also feature an arrow pointing downward at their right edges (see Figure 5-12).

Figure 5-12 A multi-window taskbar button for WordPad.

Clicking the multi-window taskbar button opens a menu listing the names of all the files and documents currently open in the program; click an entry in the list to move its window to the fore. To get a handle on using a multi-window taskbar button, do the following (again, these steps assume your desktop looks like the one shown in Figure 5-11):

❶ Click the **start** button, point to **All Programs**, point to **Accessories**, and then click **WordPad**. The WordPad window opens.

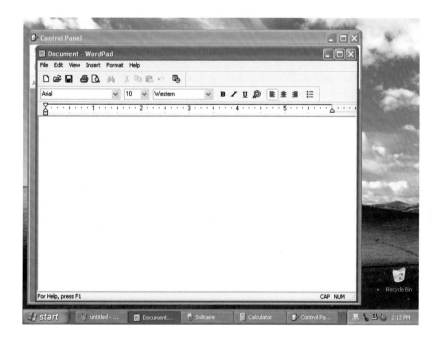

2 Repeat Step 1. Your desktop should now contain three separate program windows for WordPad stacked on top of each other.

3 Click the **WordPad** taskbar button. A menu appears, displaying the names of the documents open in each WordPad window.

4 Click the top document in the menu. The corresponding WordPad window becomes active and appears in front of all other windows.

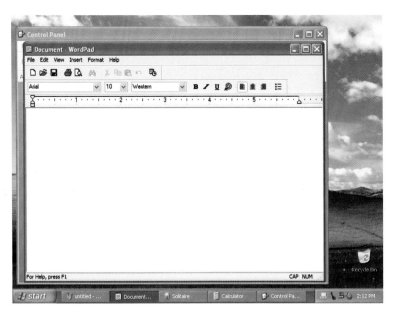

5 Close all open WordPad windows except one (click the **Close** button in the upper-right corner of each window).

Pressing the ALT+TAB Keyboard Shortcut

Another way to switch between open programs is to use the ALT+TAB keyboard shortcut. Here's how:

1 Press and hold down the **ALT** key on your keyboard.

2 With the **ALT** key still pressed, press the **TAB** key once. A dialog box appears, displaying an icon for each open window on your desktop. The active window's icon is at the far left of the dialog box, and the icon to its immediate right is selected.

3 With the **ALT** key still pressed, press the **TAB** key a second time. The next icon in the dialog box is selected.

4 Continue pressing the **TAB** key until the window you want to activate is selected.

5 Release the **ALT** key. The window you selected is activated on the desktop.

Viewing Multiple Windows Simultaneously

If you are working with multiple windows at the same time, the ability to view them simultaneously can be quite helpful. For example, if you are writing an e-mail to a friend about a Web page, you could be viewing your Web browser at the same time you are composing your e-mail message.

To view multiple windows simultaneously, do the following:

1 Right-click an empty area of the taskbar.

 If numerous icon buttons populate your taskbar, finding an empty area might get tricky. Usually, however, there's just enough space between the start button and the notification area to right-click.

❷ As shown in Figure 5-13, a shortcut menu containing numerous commands opens. Choose one of the following four commands:

Figure 5-13 The taskbar shortcut menu.

✦ **Cascade Windows.** Selecting this command repositions all open windows into a cascade layout, and resizes all windows so they are the same dimensions (typically, about half the area of the screen). This layout enables you to easily switch between windows by clicking their displayed title bars or bottom-left corners. Notice that this command manipulates only those windows that have not been minimized.

✦ **Tile Windows Horizontally.** Clicking this command resizes and repositions all open windows so that they appear stacked on each other, stretched across the screen from left to right. This layout works well if you're juggling multiple document programs. For example, this makes it easier to view the content of one or two documents while you write a third. Notice that this command manipulates only those windows that have not been minimized.

✦ **Tile Windows Vertically.** Clicking this command resizes and repositions all open windows so that they appear side-by-side from the top of the screen to the bottom. Use this layout for the same reason you might choose to tile windows horizontally—it's up to you which view is easier to use. Notice that this command manipulates only those windows that have not been minimized.

Although tiling can help you display multiple windows on your screen, the usefulness of tiling decreases as the number of open windows increases. Use these commands only if the resulting window layout improves your ability to interact with several program windows simultaneously.

✦ **Show the Desktop.** Selecting this command minimizes all open windows, enabling you to access a desktop icon or perform other desktop-related operations.

To practice using these commands, do the following:

❶ Click anywhere in the **Control Panel** window to activate it.

❷ Click the Control Panel window's **Minimize** button. The window is minimized.

❸ Click anywhere in the **WordPad** window to activate it.

❹ Click the WordPad window's **Minimize** button. The window is minimized.

❺ Right-click an empty area of the taskbar.

❻ Click the **Tile Windows Vertically** command. Your screen should look similar to the one shown in Figure 5-14. Notice that the minimized windows are not tiled.

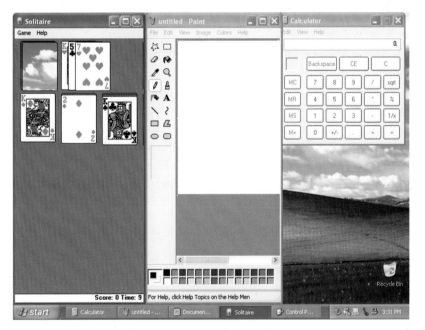

Figure 5-14 Three windows tiled vertically.

❼ After you issue a Tile command, a new command appears in the taskbar shortcut menu: Undo Tile. This command restores the open windows to their previous sizes and locations. To issue the Undo Tile command, right-click an empty area of the taskbar, and click **Undo Tile** in the shortcut menu.

❽ Right-click an empty area of the taskbar, and click the **Tile Windows Horizontally** command in the shortcut menu. Your screen should look similar to the one shown in Figure 5-15.

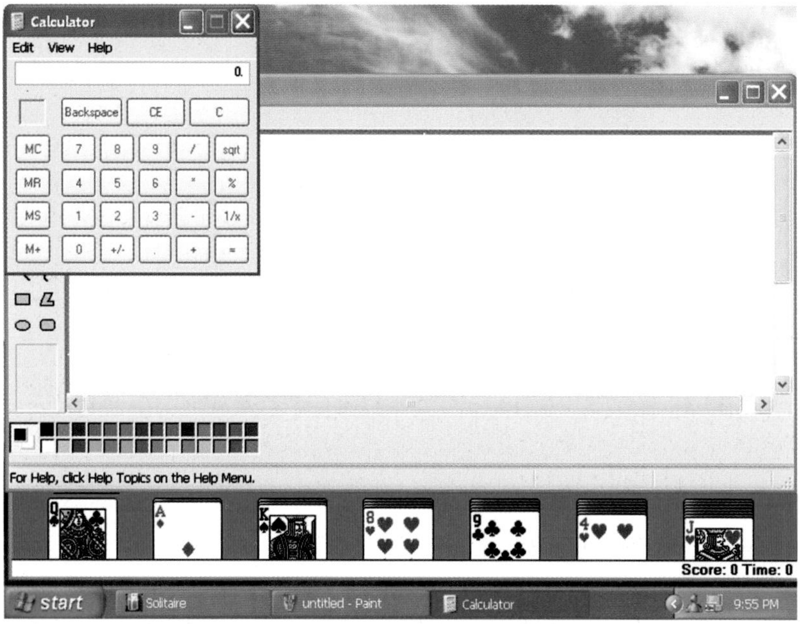

Figure 5-15 Three windows tiled horizontally.

Notice that the Calculator window overlaps the Paint window in Figure 5-15. That's because some windows have a restriction for height, width, or both. When a tiling command is issued, Windows attempts to accommodate the request. But neither the tiling command nor manual resizing can override built-in minimum display restrictions for program windows.

❾ Right-click an empty area of the taskbar, and click the **Undo Tile** command in the shortcut menu.

10 Right-click an empty area of the taskbar, and click the **Cascade Windows** command. Your screen should look similar to the one shown in Figure 5-16.

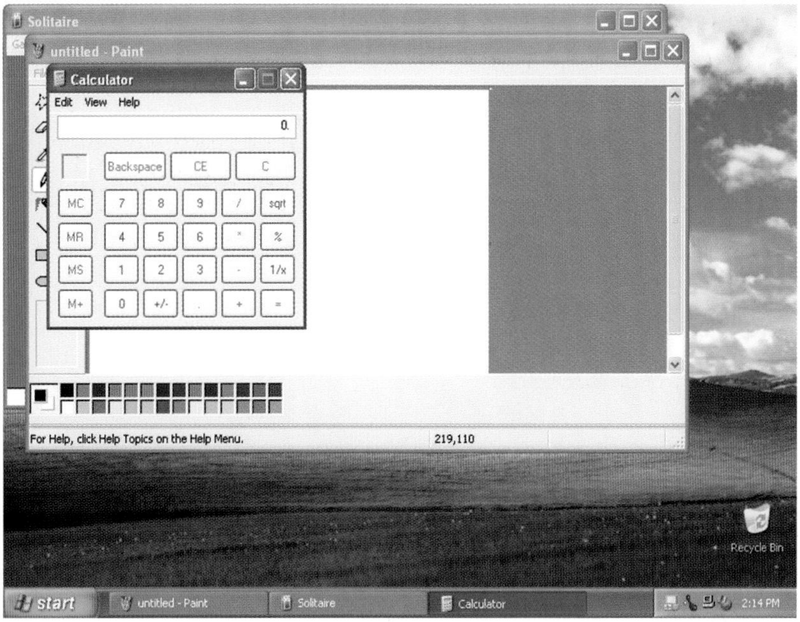

Figure 5-16 Three windows in a cascade formation.

Notice that the Calculator window is smaller than the other cascaded windows. That's because the Calculator window has built-in display restrictions that the Cascade command cannot override.

11 Just as with the Tile command, a new command appears in the taskbar shortcut menu after the Cascade command is issued: **Undo Cascade**. This command restores the open windows to their previous sizes and locations. To issue the Undo Cascade command, right-click an empty area of the taskbar, and click **Undo Cascade** in the shortcut menu.

12 Close all open windows by clicking the **Close** button in each window.

You should feel a little more comfortable working with windows, dialog boxes, wizards, and multiple windows. Keep in mind that practicing will help you fine-tune these skills.

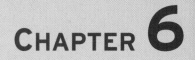

CHAPTER 6

Control Access to Your Computer

Sharing a computer with others is like sharing a desk. Each person has a favorite way to organize the paper piles and office supplies. Some people prefer a neat, orderly atmosphere, whereas others thrive in a more cluttered setting. Likewise, some computer users prefer a sparsely populated Windows desktop, while others work best on a desktop packed with their favorite shortcuts and toolbars.

Fortunately, Windows XP enables you to create separate user accounts for each person who uses your PC, enabling everyone to customize the desktop and other Windows XP features to suit their own tastes. These preferences are gathered and stored in a user profile, which includes settings that define how your desktop looks, what sounds you hear when certain events occur, and other file organizing features. This chapter shows you how to create and manage user accounts and profiles so that you and your fellow users can share a computer in harmony.

Creating and Managing User Accounts

When you install Windows XP, the setup program automatically creates a user account for you so you can start using your computer. This user account is a computer-administrator account, which gives you the ability to view and control all other user account types. When logged on as an administrator, you can create additional accounts, assign passwords to users, and limit other users' access to specific system settings and computer resources.

In addition to computer-administrator accounts, Windows XP also supports the use of limited accounts. Users with limited accounts have less power over the XP system than do users with computer-administrator accounts; with a limited account, you can change your own password, change the picture used to identify you, change Windows desktop settings, view files that you created, and view files in the Shared Documents folder.

You'll learn more about the Shared Documents folder later in this chapter.

It's a good practice to assign only one person to manage a PC using a computer-administrator account. By placing one person in charge, you prevent conflicts that naturally result whenever two or more people are in charge of the same thing. For example, one administrator might install a program on the computer one day, and the other administrator might decide to uninstall the program the next day. The sole administrator should have a separate limited account for regular PC access, and use the computer-administrator user account only when it's needed to manage the PC—that is, to install new programs or devices, change PC settings, or manage user accounts.

Adding a User Account

To create limited accounts for all the people who use your PC (including yourself), make sure you're logged on as the computer administrator. Then, do the following:

These steps assume that the computer is not networked or, if it is, it is on a peer-to-peer network, such as those used in homes and small businesses. A peer-to-peer network is a type of network in which the computers connect directly to one another rather than to a central computer. If the computer is part of a client-server network, which is managed centrally by a network administrator, the steps for adding a user account are quite different.

❶ Click the **start** button and click **Control Panel.**

❷ Control Panel opens. Click the **User Accounts** icon.

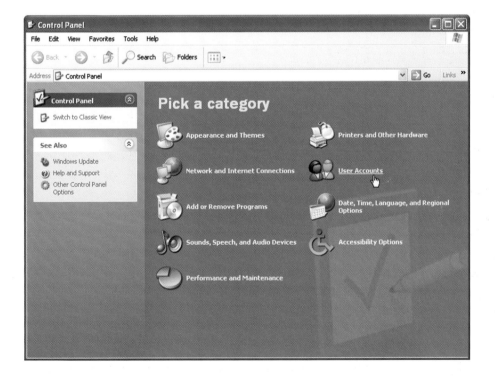

❸ The User Accounts window opens. Under Pick a task, click **Create a new account.**

❹ The Name the new account screen appears. In the **Type a name for the new account** text field, enter **Christine** for the account. It can be anything you like, as long as it contains fewer than 20 characters. Click **Next**.

❺ The Pick an account type screen appears. Click the **Limited** user account option.

❻ Click the **Create Account** button.

❼ The new user account (Christine) appears in the User Accounts window. Users are listed in alphabetical order by type of account. To create additional limited user accounts, repeat steps 3 through 6.

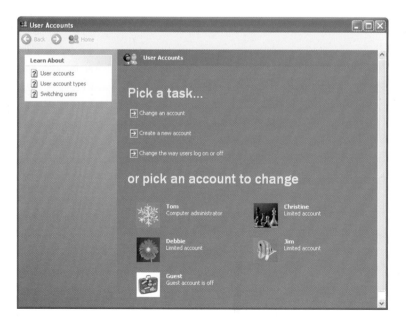

Managing User Accounts

After you've created a user account, you can change its user name, define a password, or manage any number of other aspects of the account from within the User Accounts window. (To access this window, click the **start** button and click **Control Panel**. Then, in Control Panel, click the **User Accounts** icon.)

To start, simply click the account you want to change. As shown in Figure 6-1, this opens a **What do you want to change about *x*'s account?** window, where *x* is the account's user name.

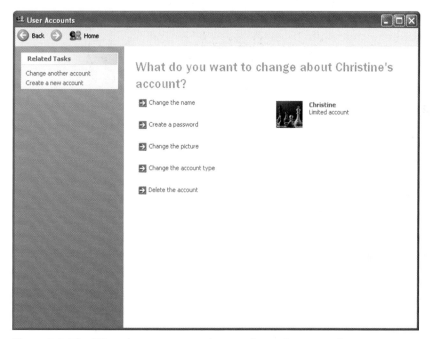

Figure 6-1 The What do you want to change about *x*'s account? screen.

Depending on what type of account you're managing (an administrator or limited account), you have various options:

✦ Change the name

✦ Create a password

✦ Change the picture

✦ Change the account type

✦ Delete the account

✦ Set up my account to use a .NET passport (administrator account only)

In the following sections, you'll learn how to perform all these tasks and enable the Guest account.

Changing a User's Name

Changing the name of a user is one of the easiest changes to make, but you must be logged on to an administrator account in order to change a user's name. If you are logged on to an administrator account, take the following steps to change your user name or the user name of another person who logs on to this computer:

1. Click the **start** button and click **Control Panel**.
2. Control Panel opens. Click the **User Accounts** icon.
3. The User Accounts window opens. Click the account whose name you want to change.
4. Windows prompts you to choose the aspect of the account you want to change. Click **Change the name**.

5. Windows highlights the current name used for this account. Type the name you want to use for this account.
6. Click the **Change Name** button. Windows changes the name and returns you to the User Accounts window.
7. Click the **Close** button.

Adding a Password to an Account

An account without a password is like a door without a lock; anyone can log on to your account and change your desktop settings or access your documents without your permission. To prevent this from happening, you should create a password for your account. When an account is password-protected, users must enter the correct password in order to log on to the account.

To password-protect your account, do the following:

1. Click the **start** button and click **Control Panel**.
2. Control Panel opens. Click the **User Accounts** icon.
3. The User Accounts window opens. Click the account you want to password-protect.
4. Windows prompts you to choose the aspect of the account you want to change. Click **Create a password**.

⑤ Windows prompts you to type a password. Do so in the **Type a new password** text box.

⑥ Type the same password a second time in the **Type the new password again to confirm** field.

⑦ In the **Type a word or phrase to use as a password hint** text box, type a hint to help you remember your password. (You can access this hint in the event you forget your password by clicking the blue question-mark box in the Welcome screen.) Remember, it should be a clue to jog your memory, not a way to share your password with others.

⑧ Click the **Create Password** button.

 Once you've defined a password for the account, a new command, Remove the password, appears on the What do you want to change about this account? screen. Use this command to remove a password from the user account.

Changing an Account's Picture

Windows assigns each user account a small picture to help identify the account graphically. You can personalize your account by selecting a picture that reflects your personality or interests. Here's how:

① Click the **start** button and click **Control Panel**.

② Control Panel opens. Click the **User Accounts** icon.

③ The User Accounts window opens. Click the account whose picture you want to change.

④ Windows prompts you to choose the aspect of the account you want to change. Click **Change the picture.**

⑤ Windows displays a collection of available images, as shown in Figure 6-2. Click the desired picture.

Figure 6-2 To personalize your user account, select a unique image.

⑥ Click the **Change Picture** button.

More About...User Account Pictures

If you have a picture on your computer's hard disk that you would rather apply to your user account, such as a digital photo or clip-art image, click the **Browse for more pictures** link in the screen shown in Figure 6-2. Windows displays the Open dialog box with the contents of the My Pictures folder in view. If your pictures are in a different disk location, navigate to the drive or folder in which the picture is stored. When you find the picture you want, click it and then click the **Open** button.

To register for
following:

1 If you are no
on now. (For
in this chapt

2 Log on to yo

3 In Windows,

4 Control Pane

5 The User Ac
obtain a .NE

6 Windows pr
account to u

7 The .NET Pa
displaying a
Read the int
click the Ne:

8 The wizard a
button.

If
lil
th

9 If your e-ma
mail addres
have a .NET

Changing the Account Type

Do you want to give another user administrator privileges or transfer your administrator responsibilities to another user? Then you need to know how to change an account type. (You can change an account type only if you are logged in as an administrator.) Here's what you do:

1 Click the **start** button and click **Control Panel**.

2 Control Panel opens. Click the **User Accounts** icon.

3 The User Accounts window opens. Click the account whose type you want to change.

4 Windows prompts you to choose the account type. Click the desired option: **Computer administrator** or **Limited**.

5 Click the **Change Account Type** button. Windows changes the account type and returns you to the User Accounts window.

6 Click the **Close** button.

Deleting a User Account

If one of the people who shares your computer moves out or buys a new machine, you can delete his or her account. Doing so removes that user's desktop settings, all the files in his or her My Documents folder, the user's e-mail messages, any sites he or she added to Internet Explorer's Favorites menu, and any passwords to Web sites that the user saved on the computer. Deleting a user account frees up space on your machine, and prevents others from accessing any of the user's information that might be confidential.

 Deleting a user account may permanently delete the user's e-mail messages and any stored passwords. Before proceeding, make absolutely sure the user wants the account deleted and doesn't need any of the information that was stored in their account.

To delete an account, do the following:

1 Click the **start** button and click **Control Panel**.

2 Control Panel opens. Click the **User Accounts** icon.

3 The User Accounts window opens. Click the account you want to delete.

4 Windows prompts you to choose the aspect of the account you want to change. Click **Delete the account**.

6

Clickin
deskto

6 Windows asks yo
you want to delet

Setting Up

.NET (pronounced
the Internet. With
installing them on
computerized devic

The .N
servic
recogn

If you have an Inte
your online identif
the Internet. Instea
you can use your .I
remember only on

Although not all o
yet, most Microsof
you must have a .N
messaging program
storage space on th

---

10 Click **Next**, then click **Next** again. Your Web browser will open, and the .NET Passport registration screen will appear.

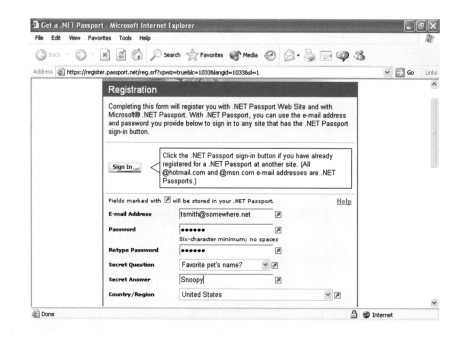

11 Type your e-mail address and type a password for your Passport account. You will need to enter the password twice – once to specify the password and the second time to confirm it. Passwords must be at least six characters long and cannot include spaces. Passwords will appear on your screen as a series of dots to prevent others from seeing your password.

Your password is case-sensitive, so remember which letters in your password are capitalized.

12 To safeguard you in the event you forget your .NET password, the .NET Passport screen asks you to select a question from the Secret Question drop-down list and type an answer in the answer text box. If you forget your password, .NET Passport verifies your identity by asking you the secret question you select here.

⑬ Enter your country, state, and ZIP code in the appropriate spaces.

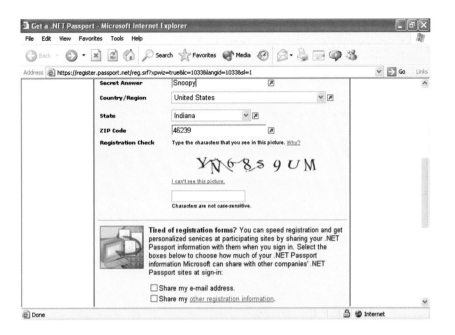

To eliminate computerized mass registrations, a registration check graphic box appears with some letters and numbers placed randomly in the box. In the text box below the graphic box, type the letters and numbers in the order you see them displayed in the graphic box. The letters are not case-sensitive.

⑭ If you want to share your e-mail address with other .NET Passport sites, click the **Share my e-mail address** box and/or the **Share my other registration information** box.

⑮ At the bottom of the window is the .NET Passport terms of use agreement. Read the agreement. If you agree to the terms, click **I Agree**.

⑯ The .NET Passport Wizard informs you that you have successfully registered. Click **Continue**, and then click **Finish**.

Enabling Guest Accounts

If a person occasionally uses your PC, but not often enough to require the creation of a separate user account, you can set up Windows to allow that user to log on as a guest. With a guest account, users can log on without a password, run programs, check e-mail, and browse the Web, but cannot install software or change the account settings.

To set up the guest account, take the following steps:

❶ Click the **start** button and click **Control Panel**.

❷ Control Panel opens. Click the **User Accounts** icon.

❸ The User Accounts window appears. Click the **Guest** icon.

❹ The screen shown in Figure 6-3 appears. Click the **Turn On the Guest Account** button. You return to the User Accounts window, which indicates that the Guest account is on. Users can now log on as guests.

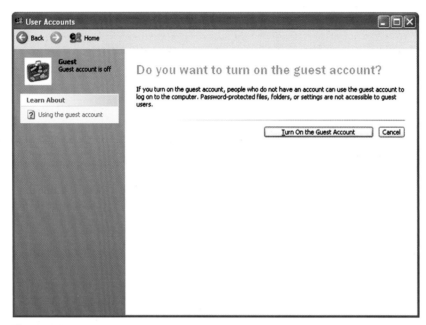

Figure 6-3 Turn on the guest account to allow any user to log on without a user name or password.

Logging Off and Switching Accounts

User accounts can protect each user's settings and files only if each person logs on using his or her own user account and logs off of that account when finished using the computer. If a user steps away from the computer without logging off, anyone can use the open account. That's why it's important to log off an account or switch users whenever you're done using the computer. In the following sections, you learn how to log off your computer and how to switch users without logging off.

To find out which user is currently logged on to Windows, click the **start** button. At the top of the start menu is a bar that displays the name of the user who is currently logged on.

Logging Off Windows

If you are finished using your computer, or you want to step away from it for a while but don't want others to access your user account, you can log off. The logoff process closes your user account and returns you to the logon screen.

 Before you log off, save any documents you have open on your desktop. However, you need not quit open programs. Windows automatically shuts down these programs when you log off.

When you are ready to log off, do the following:

❶ Click the **start** button, and then click **Log Off**.

❷ The Log Off Windows dialog box opens. Click the **Log Off** button to log off your user account and return to the logon screen.

Switching Users Without Logging Off

Suppose you're balancing the family's electronic checkbook on your PC, but your daughter needs to quickly look something up on the Internet in order to complete her homework. Using the Windows XP Fast User Switching feature, your daughter can log on without requiring you to log off first. You can leave all your programs open, switch users, let her find the information for her homework, and then switch back to your desktop—without losing any of your work! (Before you switch users, it's a good idea to save any documents currently open on your desktop.)

 Only the capabilities of the PC itself limit the number of user accounts that can be logged on simultaneously using Fast User Switching. The more memory and CPU power a system has, the better it can support multiple users at any given time. However, we recommend that you not push this feature to its limits. As a general rule, it's wise to stick with three or fewer users logged on at any given time.

Fast User Switching is active by default on computers that have more than 64 megabytes (MB) of RAM. (Fast User Switching is not available on networked computers that are part of a domain.)

To quickly switch users, do the following:

1 Click the **start** button, and then click **Log Off**.

2 The Log Off Windows dialog box opens. Click the **Switch User** button.

 When you switch accounts using Fast User Switching, your desktop is hidden, but your open programs continue to run. For example, if you are in the process of downloading a file and you use Fast User Switching to switch user accounts, that activity continues even though your desktop is hidden.

3 The Windows Welcome screen appears; notice that it displays the number of programs currently running on the open user account. To log on to another user account, click its icon in the Windows Welcome screen and enter the account's password if one is required.

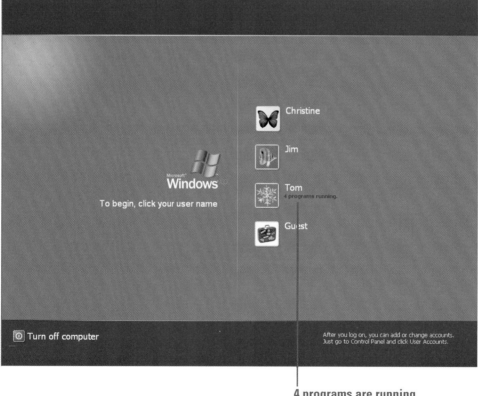

**4 programs are running
under the user Tom**

When the other user finishes using her user account, she can log out. This displays the Windows Welcome screen; simply click your user account to reopen your desktop. You'll find everything running just the way you left it.

 If multiple users log in through Fast User Switching and a problem occurs that can only be fixed by a restart, you may not be able to log out each of the user accounts gracefully. Unfortunately, this means that any data not already saved into a file is lost. If you are concerned about this happening to your system, you can deactivate Fast User Switching. To do so, follow the steps you took to set up this feature, but click the **Use Fast User Switching** check box to deselect it.

Keeping Your Documents Private

Whenever you create a user account, Windows creates a folder called "My Documents," in which you can save all the documents you create. That's right—each user account gets its own folder called "My Documents." So how do you tell the difference between your My Documents folder and another user's My Documents folder? Well, Windows does a little behind-the-scenes work to help distinguish between folders of the same name. Say your name is Christine, and you log on to your user account; your folder appears to you as My Documents. When you want to open one of your documents, you go to the My Documents folder. Now, say Tom logs on to the computer and wants to open a document in your folder. When Tom logs on to the computer, your folder appears as Christine's Documents, and Tom's folder is labeled My Documents.

If you store a diary or other confidential documents on your computer, you probably don't want your family members or co-workers to read them. Fortunately, Windows allows you to block access to your My Documents folder and all of its contents by making the folder a private folder.

 You cannot make a folder a private folder unless you add a password to your account.

To designate My Documents as a private folder, do the following:

1 Click the **start** button and then click the **My Computer** icon.

2 The My Computer window opens, displaying icons for the available drives. Double-click the icon for the drive on which Windows is installed (typically C:).

3 My Computer displays the contents of drive C:. Double-click the **Documents and Settings** folder.

4 My Computer displays the contents of the Documents and Settings folder, which consists of a folder for each user account. Double-click the folder for your user account.

Make this folder private

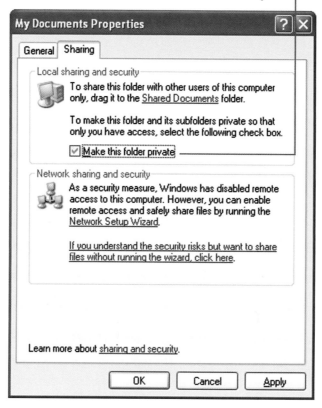

5 My Computer displays the contents of your user-account folder. You can block access to any of the folders here. To do so, right-click the **My Documents** folder. In the shortcut menu that appears, click **Sharing and Security**.

6 The My Documents Properties dialog box opens, with the Sharing tab displayed. Click **Make this folder private** and click **OK**. (The Make this folder private option only works for user accounts that require a password to log on.) If a user doesn't have a password, anyone can log on with the user name and access the folder.

Now that you've locked your confidential files in a safe place, how do you provide access to those files if you change your mind later? Simply turn off the Make this folder private setting. Here's what you do:

1. Return to the Documents and Settings folder (click **start**, click **My Computer**, double-click the drive C: icon, and then double-click the **Documents and Settings** folder).

2. Double-click the folder for your user account, and then click the **My Documents** folder.

3. On the left side of the My Computer window, in File and Folder Tasks, click **Share This Folder**.

4. The My Documents Properties dialog box opens, with the Sharing tab displayed. Click **Make this folder private** (to clear the check box) and click **OK**.

6

Let's Get Organized

O ur lives are full and busy, and to keep ourselves organized, we often write down our schedules on a calendar, store addresses and phone numbers in an address book, and keep our keys on the same hook by the door so we can find them quickly. The same is true with your computer; you'll end up creating lots of different files, and you need some pattern to organize them so you can locate the file you want quickly and easily. Windows uses folders, subfolders, and disk drives to help you keep track of those critical (and maybe some not so critical) pieces of information. This chapter will show you how to organize and store your work.

Creating Folders and Subfolders

Chances are, you use a filing cabinet at work or at home to organize important papers and other items. Like a filing cabinet, your PC's hard disk enables you to "file" your important documents. You can do so in your My Documents folder, which acts like a drawer in a filing cabinet. You can even create and label your own set of folders within this "drawer"; this lets you organize the documents, or files, you create using your PC. You can even create subfolders and place them inside other folders. In an organized folder structure, you can locate your documents easily.

Follow these steps to create a folder and subfolder in My Documents:

1 Click the start button, and then click My Documents. The My Documents window opens.

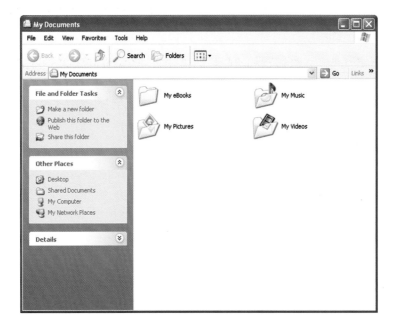

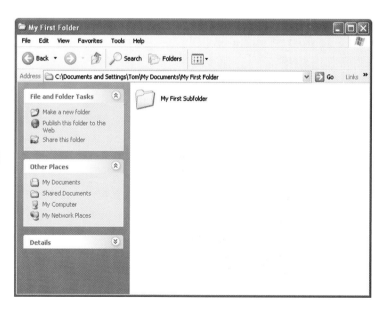

2 Under File and Folder Tasks, click Make a new folder. A new folder icon appears in the window, with the name "New Folder" selected.

3 Type My First Folder, and press ENTER. This replaces the name "New Folder" with "My First Folder."

4 Position your mouse pointer over the new folder. A ToolTip appears, telling you that the folder is empty.

5 Double-click My First Folder. The title of the window changes from "My Documents" to "My First Folder."

6 Under File and Folder Tasks, click Make a new folder. A new folder icon appears in the My First Folder window with the name "New Folder" selected.

7 Type My First Subfolder, and press ENTER. This replaces the name "New Folder" with "My First Subfolder."

8 Click the Back button twice to return to the My Documents window.

9 Place your mouse over My First Folder. The ToolTip now lists the subfolder you just created as the contents of this folder.

10 Click the Close button to close the My Documents window and return to the desktop.

Creating New Files

Making a new file in your programs can be accomplished in a few different ways. Your computer gives you options of how to create new documents that you can save in order to access them at a later time. You can choose which way works best for you.

Creating and Saving a File Using a Program

To create a simple file using a program (in this case, WordPad), do the following:

1. Click the start button, point to All Programs, point to Accessories, and click WordPad.
2. The WordPad program starts, displaying a window labeled "Document – WordPad".

3. The blinking vertical bar (called the insertion point) in the upper-left corner of the workspace indicates where text will appear when you start typing. Type This is my first new document using Microsoft Windows XP and WordPad. Notice that the insertion point moves across the page as you type.
4. Click File in the menu bar, and then click Save. Notice that the Save As dialog box opens (you'll learn about why this happens in the next section).

Save As dialog box showing Save in: My Documents, with folders My eBooks, My First Folder, My Music, My Pictures, My Videos. File name: Document.rtf. Save as type: Rich Text Format (RTF). Save in this format by default. Labels point to "Save in list" and "Save button."

5. In the Save in list, find the folder named "My First Folder" (remember, it's in My Documents). When you locate My First Folder, double-click it so it opens up. (The folder icon to the left changes from a closed folder to an open one.)

6. In the File name text box, double-click the default entry Document to highlight that name, and then type My New File. This is how you replace a default name for the file with the name you actually want to use.

7. Click the Save button to save the document, close the Save As dialog box, and return to the WordPad window. Notice that the name of the file, "My New File," now appears in the title bar at the top of the screen.

8. Click the Close button to close the WordPad window and return to the desktop.

Creating a File with the Shortcut Menu

Depending on the number of programs installed on a PC, sometimes navigating the All Programs menu can be cumbersome. Luckily, there's another way to start programs and create files—using the shortcut menu that appears when you right-click your desktop. Follow these steps to create a file using this method:

1. Right-click a blank area of your desktop.

Arrange Icons By ▶	
Refresh	
Paste	
Paste Shortcut	
Undo Rename Ctrl+Z	
New ▶	🗀 Eolder
Properties	🗿 Shortcut

🖼 Briefcase
🖼 Bitmap Image
📝 Microsoft Word Document
📄 Microsoft Access Application
📄 Microsoft PowerPoint Presentation
📄 Microsoft Publisher Document
📄 Text Document
🎙 wav file
📊 Microsoft Excel Worksheet
🗜 Compressed (zipped) Folder

② A shortcut menu appears. Point to New to reveal the New submenu.

③ Click Text Document. A new text document icon appears on the desktop with the name "New Text Document" selected.

④ Type My First Text Doc, and press ENTER. The name "New Text Document" is replaced with the name you typed.

⑤ Double-click the My First Text Doc icon on your desktop. The Notepad program starts and the My First Text Doc – Notepad window opens.

⑥ Type This is my second new document using Microsoft Windows XP.

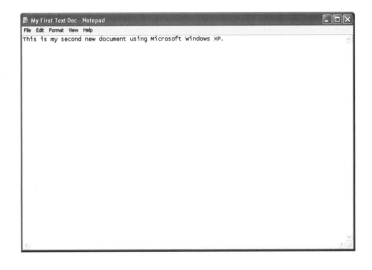

⑦ Click File in the menu bar, and then click Save. Because you have already named this document (My First Text Doc), and saved it to a location (the desktop), no Save As dialog box opens.

⑧ Click the Close button to close the Notepad window and return to the desktop.

Opening a File

In Windows XP, the act of opening a file often involves navigating within the folders, subfolders, and files in the file system. As you work your way through the various ways to open files, you'll see that in many cases, part of what's involved is locating and pointing to a file so you can instruct a program to do something with it. Keep this in mind as you read the sections that follow.

Opening a File Using a Program

Once you start a program, you can use its built-in file handling capabilities to open existing files that you want to work on. You can always use the program's built-in menus to do this, but in most cases, you can also click a toolbar icon to do the same thing. Here's an example using menus in WordPad (click start, then All Programs, then Accessories, then WordPad to open that program):

1. Click the File button in the menu bar. The File menu appears.
2. Click Open in the File menu. The Open dialog box opens.

3. This should open with My First Folder in the Look in list, because that's where you left off last time. If not, navigate through My Documents to My First Folder. This displays the contents of that folder in the item display area below the list.
4. Select the My New File icon in the item display area, and then click the Open button. This opens your file in WordPad's workspace. You're ready to go to work!

7

5 To prepare for the next exercise, close WordPad by clicking the **Close** button.

 To perform the same actions covered in the preceding steps using the toolbar Open button, simply skip steps 1 and 2, and click the **Open** button on the program's toolbar instead. Replacing two steps with one explains why this is a good approach.

That's how you open files when you're already running some particular program. If you're starting work in a program that's not already running, there's another way to get to work. It involves using the icon that represents the file you want to work on, and is explained in the next section.

Opening a File Using the File Icon

Opening the My First Text Doc file is easy, because you saved it to the desktop. Simply locate its icon on your desktop and double-click that icon to open the file inside Notepad. This same principle works for other files as long as you can find the icon for a file to double-click it. Also, Windows must recognize what program to use with the file (we talk about what that means later in this chapter in the section titled "Managing File Associations").

Here's how to open your text document by clicking its file icon:

1 Close any open applications so you can see your desktop. Notice the My First Text Doc icon on your desktop.

② Double-click the My First Text Doc icon to open that document.

③ The document opens in Notepad, ready for you to get to work. Note how easy and convenient it is to open a file from the desktop!

```
My First Text Doc - Notepad
File  Edit  Format  View  Help
This is my second new document using Microsoft Windows XP.
```

④ Click the Close button to exit Notepad.

Working with Removable Media

If you want to share data with others and you're not on a network or connected to the Internet, you'll need to use some type of removable media. In this section, we will work with two of the removable media types you learned about in Chapter 1; floppy disks and USB flash drives.

Using Floppy Disks

Floppy disks are handy as they are small and easily portable. However, they are designed to allow you to store a small file or two, since each floppy diskette can hold only about 1.44 MB of data. Many newer PCs do not have a floppy disk drive, but if your PC is two or more years old, you probably have one on your system. Just like your computer hard drive is assigned the letter C:, as you can see in the My Computer window seen in Figure 7-1, your computer refers to the 3 ½ Floppy as the A: drive.

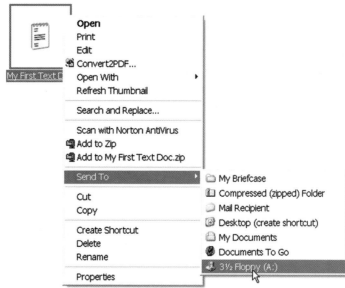

Figure 7-1 Your computer always assigns floppy disk drives the drive letter A:.

The following steps illustrate how to copy a file to a floppy disk:

1. Insert a blank formatted disk into the floppy disk drive in the front of your PC. Insert the metal end first; the solid side of the disk is the top. Push the disk securely into the drive until you hear a light snap sound.

2. Open the folder that contains the file you want to copy. The folder might be the My Documents folder, your Windows desktop, or any other folder you specify.

3. Locate the file you want to copy to the floppy disk, right-click on it, then click **Send To** from the shortcut menu that appears. Click **3 ½ Floppy (A:)** from the submenu to save the selected file to the floppy disk.

To check if the file is safely stored on the floppy disk, from the start menu, click **My Computer** then double-click the **3 ½ (A:)** icon to display the contents of the floppy disk.

 It's a good idea to remove disks from the floppy disk drive immediately after use. If you leave a diskette in the floppy drive, then restart your computer, it can interfere with the operating system startup.

Using USB Flash Drives

7

Flash drives are becoming more popular every day because they can store a relatively large amount of data in a small device. Flash drives come in a variety of sizes, from 32 MB of storage (compared to 1.44 MB on a floppy disk) up to a whopping 1 GB of storage. Flash drives plug into a USB port on your computer.

Aside from the difference in storage capacity, flash drives are managed similarly to floppy drives. The main difference is the drive letter. While floppy disk drives are always considered the A: drive, USB Flash drives are typically assigned the next available alphabetic letter depending on your current system hardware. In Figure 7-2, you can see where the system has assigned the letter Removable Disk (F:), as F was the next available drive letter.

Figure 7-2 When you insert your flash drive, an icon appears for it on the My Computer screen.

Copying a file to a USB Flash Drive is very similar to copying a file to a floppy disk. Follow these steps:

❶ Plug the drive into an open USB port. Newer PCs have USB ports on both the front and back, while slightly older PCs may only have USB ports on the back of the system. PCs five years and older may not have USB ports.

❷ Open the folder that contains the file you want to copy. The folder might be the My Documents folder, your Windows desktop, or any other folder you specify.

❸ Locate the file you want to copy to the floppy disk, right-click on it, then click **Send To** from the shortcut menu that appears.

❹ Click **Removable Disk (F:)** or whatever letter your computer has assigned to your flash drive. Windows will copy the selected file to the flash drive.

To confirm the file is safely stored on the flash drive, from the start menu, click **My Computer**, then double-click the **Removable Disk (F:)** icon to display the contents of the flash drive.

To open a file from a floppy drive or a flash drive, locate the file through the appropriate drive letter in My Computer, then double-click the file to open it in its originating program.

Managing File Associations

By now, you've probably noticed that nearly all Windows files have associated types. For example, type names appear in the Save as type list box in a Save As dialog box. In file names, file types are expressed as file name extensions, which are groups of three or more characters that appear to the right of the rightmost period in a file name. Windows uses this information to decide which programs to use with particular files.

By default, Windows XP hides these characters when it shows you icons for files and other objects. You can see them if you alter your folder options in My Computer or Windows Explorer and instruct the software to show you that information. Here's how:

1 Click start and click My Documents. This lists that folder's contents.

2 Double-click My First Folder. This lists its contents, including My New File.

3 Click Tools and click Folder Options in the Tools menu. The Folder Options window opens.

4 Click the View tab to look at its contents, and then clear the Hide extensions for known file types check box. Click OK to close the Folder Options dialog box.

5 You should now see My New File.rtf as the file name in the My First Folder listing.

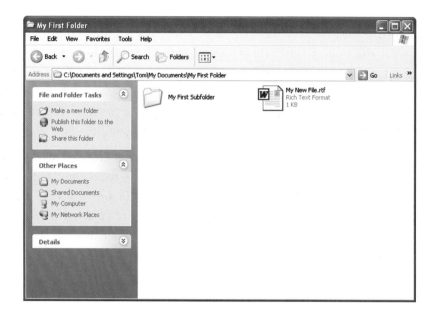

6 Click **Tools**, click **Folder Options**, click the **View** tab, and then click the **Restore Defaults** button to return to the original settings. Click **OK** to close the dialog box.

7 Click the **Close** button to close the My First Folder window.

Windows XP associates the file extension .rtf with WordPad and Microsoft Word as well. On machines where both programs are installed, double-clicking a file with an .rtf extension opens Word, not WordPad, because it is a preferred file association.

In the sections that follow, we explain how files and folders work in the Windows XP environment, and how you can create and organize your own folders to help you find files when you need them.

Working with Files and Folders

When you start working with multiple programs or creating lots of individual files, a single folder really can't provide sufficient organization to help you keep track of your many separate interests and activities—and the files that go with them. Nor does it make sense to mix up your collection of music lyric files with your monthly checkbook statements. That's why creating your own collection of folders is so important.

Organized Files Need Folder Structures

Getting your PC organized means understanding what kinds of programs you use, what kinds of files you work with, and what kinds of activities you conduct. All of these elements can help guide how you organize folders on your hard drive. This organization should build from a relatively small set of primary activities at the highest level (those folders that contain the most subfolders) to an increasingly large set of individual, specific activities within the primary folders as the number of levels goes up.

Let's walk through an example to illustrate this concept. Nearly every person or family must deal with financial matters to handle the demands of everyday life. It's predictable that many PCs could include a Finances folder, as shown in Figure 7-3, that appears at the top level of Local Disk (C:). Within the Finances folder, you'd organize various aspects of your financial life. Let's assume that this set of folders makes sense for our hypothetical personal or family PC.

Figure 7-3 Finances folder.

In this sample illustration, it's pretty clear that Tom and Christine have their finances well in hand. They've got categories for all kinds of forward-looking money, including College Fund (for their grandchildrens' college funds), Investments, Savings, Retirement, and even Vacation Fund. In addition, they've got the everyday basics covered, including a household Budget folder, Checkbooks, Credit Cards, Loans, and Taxes. What's important to note is that they've set up a collection of folders (with files inside them) that mirrors the various activities and individual people or items that must be tracked separately. For example, that explains why the contents of the Loans folder include a 98-Explorer folder (for Christine's car) and a 99-Focus folder (for Tom's car).

Once you have a sizable collection of files and folders to manage, as our Finances example shows, you must get comfortable navigating within that collection. That's why we talk about folder navigation next.

Navigating Folder Structures

When it comes to moving around inside folder structures that are four or more levels deep, basic navigational skills are essential. To that end, certain tools and techniques can be extremely handy. We cover these in the paragraphs that follow.

Build a mental map: If you create an organization, it should be one that makes sense to you. This will help you to keep a mental image of the folder structure in your head. Continued use and access will make this structure familiar to you.

Visual exploration: When you open one folder, look at what's inside. Check out the files that reside there. Then systematically open each subfolder, and keep going until you've seen it all—or as much as you need to know right now.

Use Back and Up buttons: The Back and Up buttons take you back to your previous location and make good tools for systematic exploration of folder structures.

Searching strategies: When you can't remember a folder structure but you know certain characteristics for the file or folder you seek, use the Windows XP Search Companion to find what you need.

In the next section, we explore some of the tools and techniques you can use to inspect files within any given folder. It's a good idea to create a restore point, as we will be changing folder views. That way, after you complete the next few sections, you can choose to reset Windows XP to exactly how it looks now.

Changing the Folder View

A Windows Explorer window is split into two sections, as shown in Figure 7-4. The left side of the window displays either a series of lists (list pane), or a hierarchical listing of everything stored on your PC (folders pane). The right side of the window, called the details pane, displays the contents of a folder or drive.

To open Windows Explorer, click start, right-click My Documents, and then click Explore in the shortcut menu. There are six ways to view the details pane. (This applies to normal folder views as well.) Click the Views button on the toolbar to display each view.

✦ **Tiles view.** Displays files and folders as large icons with sorted information underneath; displayed by default the first time you open Windows Explorer.

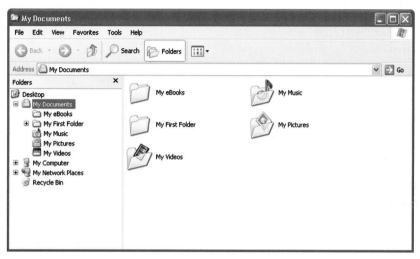

Figure 7-4 Windows Explorer.

✦ **Thumbnails view.** Handy for folders that contain pictures; displays four contained images or icons within the folder icon itself.

◆ **Icons view.** Displays files and folders as icons (small graphical representations).

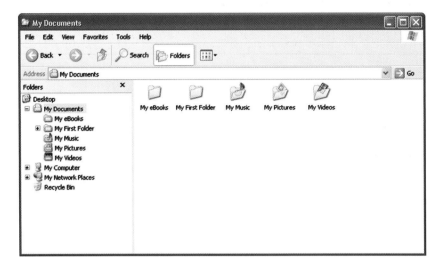

◆ **List view.** Displays the contents of a folder or drive in a list, in which each item is preceded by a small icon.

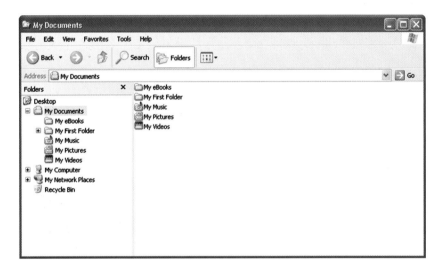

◆ **Details view.** Looks like the List view, but adds type, size, and date modified information. Sort this view with a single click on any column name (click once for ascending order, again for descending).

◆ **Filmstrip view.** Available only for picture folders; displays images in a single row (like a filmstrip).

Sorting the Details View

When Details view is selected in Windows Explorer, a broad range of information about each item in the selected drive or folder is available. Not only are the contents of the drive displayed, but also the size and type of each file in the drive, as well as the date each file was last modified. You can sort the contents of this window using any one of these characteristics (size, type, date modified) in ascending or descending order. For example, you might sort the files on your C: drive by file type to quickly locate files generated by a certain program.

To determine which characteristic is currently being used to sort the items in the selected drive or folder, check the column headings. The heading with an arrow next to it indicates the characteristic being used to sort the files; the direction of the arrow indicates whether files are being sorted in ascending or descending order. For example, suppose the Name column heading has an upward-pointing arrow next to it (see Figure 7-5). That indicates that items in the details pane are being sorted in ascending order by file name.

Name ▲

Figure 7-5 Name column heading in Details view.

To learn how to sort your files in Details view, do the following:

1. In Windows Explorer, navigate to My First Folder in My Documents. Click the Views button on the toolbar and click Details.

2. Click the Size column heading. The items in the selected drive are sorted from smallest to largest, with folders at the top of the list.

③ Click the Size column heading again. The items in the selected drive are sorted from largest to smallest, with files at the top of the list.

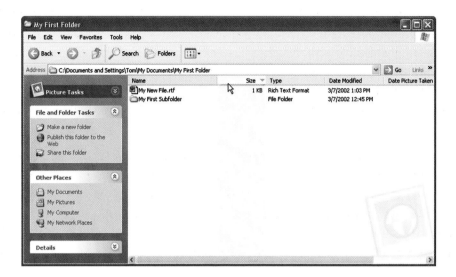

④ Click the Type column heading to sort the items in the selected drive in ascending order by file type; click Type again to sort the items in descending order.

⑤ Click the Date Modified column heading to sort the items in the selected drive in ascending order by date; click Date Modified again to sort the items in descending order.

⑥ Click the Name column heading to sort the items in the selected drive in ascending order by file name.

⑦ Click the Close button to close the Local Disk (C:) window.

As you learn how to view and sort files to help you find what you're looking for, you'll start to appreciate the power and flexibility of the Details view. Soon, it should become second nature to you.

Now that you're familiar with Windows Explorer and have changed many different settings, you can restore your PC to the way it looked and behaved before you began. To do so, however, you must have created a restore point as instructed in the "Navigating Folder Structures" section.

7

Paths and Shortcuts: Know Where You're Going

In Chapter 7, you learned how to create folders and subfolders to store and organize your files. Now that you have all these files, folders, programs, and other things on your computer, you may have the need to change the files' or folders' location, name, or other attribute. This chapter will help you manage these objects and their properties.

Understanding Object Paths

When you send a letter to someone, you write the recipient's name and address on the envelope to ensure that the letter is delivered to the correct person. The same way an object—be it a file, a folder, a printer, or some other Windows resource—uses a unique "address" to identify it among all other resources on a PC, even those of the same type and name. That way, it can always be located and accessed properly. The secret to this addressing scheme is called an object path. An object path uses all the location information necessary to identify any object's exact location as a prefix to that object's name.

To illustrate, let's find a concrete example of an object path using Windows Explorer:

1 Click **start**. The start menu appears.

2 Right-click **My Computer**, and then select **Explore** from the shortcut menu that appears. The My Computer window opens in Windows Explorer format.

Windows Explorer enables you to view files and folders stored on any disk on your computer and see any network drives accessible from your computer.

3 Double-click the **Local Disk (C:)** icon in the details pane (the pane on the right). My Computer displays the top-level folders on the Local Disk (C:) along with any files in the current folder.

4 Double-click the **Documents and Settings** folder icon. My Computer displays a list of folders related to users defined on your PC.

5 Double-click the **All Users** folder icon. My Computer lists folders associated with any user who logs on to your system.

All Users

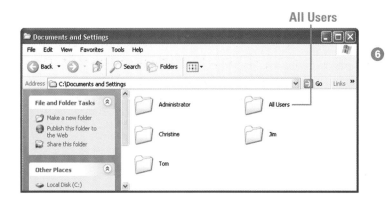

6 Double-click the **Start Menu** folder icon. My Computer lists elements in the default start menu for all users, including the Windows Catalog and Windows Update shortcuts.

Note the text that appears in the **Address** box in the My Computer window: It reads **C:\Documents and Settings\All Users\Start Menu**. This is the object path for objects that reside inside the Start Menu folder. When you combine this information with an object's name, you have the complete address for the object. For example, the complete addresses for the Windows Catalog and Windows Update shortcuts inside the Start Menu folder are:

✦ C:\Documents and Settings\All Users\Start Menu\Windows Catalog

✦ C:\Documents and Settings\All Users\Start Menu\Windows Update

Creating and Managing Shortcuts

8

In the preceding section, you discovered the object path to two shortcuts that appear in Windows Explorer by default: Windows Catalog and Windows Update. A shortcut is a kind of Windows XP object that enables you to associate an icon on the desktop or in some other convenient location with a specific document, program, printer, or other resource.

Although a shortcut can be placed just about anywhere you like, the most common and most convenient location for shortcuts is the Windows XP desktop. For example, suppose you frequently use WordPad. To launch it, you click start, then All Programs, then Accessories, then WordPad. That's a total of four mouse clicks. To save time and effort, you could place a shortcut to WordPad on your desktop. That way, you could simply double-click the shortcut to launch the program.

Shortcuts look like ordinary program icons, but with a small arrow in a box in the lower-left corner. Figure 8-1 shows a desktop shortcut to WordPad; you'll learn how to create one for yourself in the next section.

Figure 8-1 WordPad shortcut icon.

Note that shortcuts are part of each user's desktop environment. If Tom and Christine both have accounts on a Windows XP PC, Tom's shortcuts show up only when he logs on, and Christine's only when she logs on. As you work with shortcuts, you can drag and drop them onto the start menu (or its submenus).

Creating a Shortcut to a Program, Drive, or Folder

There are many ways to create shortcuts in the Windows XP environment; the following are just a few:

1. One is to right-click and drag the program, drive, folder, or other object from the My Computer window (or other location) to the desktop and select Create Shortcut Here from the menu that appears.

2. You can also drag items from the start menu to the desktop.

The method illustrated here uses a right-click and drag operation to create a program shortcut (in this case, for WordPad):

❶ Click start. The start menu opens.

❷ Click All Programs. A list of programs on your PC appears.

❸ Click Accessories to view a list of accessory-type programs installed on your computer.

❹ Click WordPad and, while holding down your mouse button, drag the icon from the menu to your desktop.

❺ Release the mouse button to "drop" the WordPad icon on your desktop. A shortcut menu appears.

❻ Click Copy Here to create a shortcut on the desktop.

❼ Double-click the shortcut. Windows XP starts WordPad, displaying the WordPad program window on your desktop. Click the Close button in the upper-right corner to close this window.

Another way to create a shortcut, whether it's for a program or another type of object, is to use the Create Shortcut Wizard. Here's how:

 If you complete the steps here in addition to the ones immediately preceding, you will end up with three WordPad icons on your desktop. This doesn't cause any problems with your system, but consumes valuable desktop space. Fortunately, you'll learn how to delete shortcuts and other objects later in this chapter.

1 Right-click an empty area on the desktop, click **New** in the shortcut menu that appears, and then click **Shortcut**. The Create Shortcut Wizard starts.

2 Click the **Browse** button to locate the object for which you want to create a shortcut. The Browse For Folder dialog box opens.

3 Click the **WordPad** shortcut icon, and then click **OK**.

4 The object's path appears in the wizard screen. Click **Next** to continue.

5 Windows XP provides a default name for the shortcut. To change it, you could type a preferred name over the default. In this case, leave the default name of "wordpad (2)."

6 Click **Finish**. A shortcut named "wordpad (2)" appears on your desktop.

7 Repeat steps 1 through 6 to create a "wordpad (3)" shortcut on your desktop.

8 Double-click one of the new shortcuts. Windows XP starts WordPad, displaying the WordPad program window on your desktop. Click the **Close** button in the upper-right corner to close this window.

Create Shortcut

This wizard helps you to create shortcuts to local or network programs, files, folders, computers, or Internet addresses.

Type the location of the item:

[   ] Browse...

Click Next to continue.

< Back   Next >   Cancel

Select a Title for the Program

Type a name for this shortcut:

[wordpad (2)]

Click Finish to create the shortcut.

< Back   Finish   Cancel

8

Creating a Shortcut to a File

Suppose you've decided to write your memoirs—a project that could take you weeks, months, or even years to complete. That means you'll be opening the same word-processing file to compose your masterpiece every single day for the foreseeable future. To save yourself time each day, you can create a shortcut to that file; that way, you can open the file and the word-processing program you use to work on it in one easy step.

In this example, you'll create a file in WordPad, and then create a shortcut to access it from the desktop:

1 Double-click the **WordPad** shortcut icon on the desktop. WordPad starts, and its program window opens on your desktop.

2 In the WordPad work area, type **My book begins with this simple sentence.**

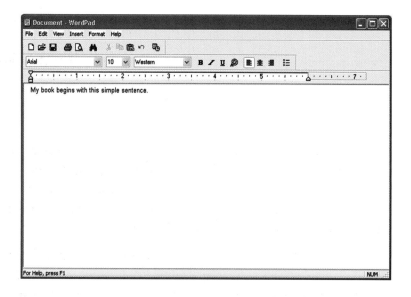

3 Click the **Save** toolbar button (the one with a picture of a floppy disk on it). The Save As dialog box opens.

4 Double-click **My Documents** and double-click **My First Folder**. Type **MyBook** in the File name text box and click the **Save** button.

5 Click the **Close** button to close the WordPad window.

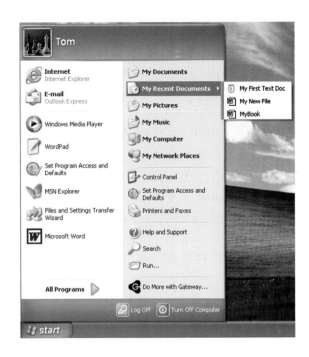

6 Click **start** and click **My Recent Documents** to view a list of documents you've accessed recently.

7 In the list of documents, right-click **MyBook**, click **Send to** in the shortcut menu that appears, and click **Desktop (create shortcut)** in the Send to submenu. A shortcut for the file appears on the desktop.

8 Click the **Close** button to close the My First Folder window.

Using the Desktop Cleanup Wizard

The more shortcuts you create and the more programs you install, the more likely it is that their icons begin to overwhelm your Windows XP desktop, cluttering your workspace. Of course, one way to rein in this clutter is to delete shortcuts you no longer use; then again, you can almost guarantee that the second you delete a shortcut, something will happen to make you wish it was still on your desktop.

As an alternative to deleting shortcuts, you can use the Desktop Cleanup Wizard. This wizard analyzes the shortcuts on your desktop to determine the last time each one was used. Any shortcuts that haven't been used for a while are moved to a desktop folder called "Unused Desktop Shortcuts." Here they are stored safely in case you need them again without consuming valuable desktop real estate.

8

Manipulating Objects

One of the great things about Windows XP is how easily it allows you to manipulate the objects on your system. Do you want to copy or move a file from one folder to another? No problem. Are you finished using an object? You can easily delete it. You can also rename, open, and even print objects. Before you can manipulate the objects on your PC, however, you must learn how to select them. This section demonstrates how to select objects, and addresses all the important things you can do with objects.

In Chapter 7, you were instructed to create several folders, subfolders, and files; these same objects are used in the exercises that follow. If you did not create these objects, you can substitute folders, subfolders, and files of your own.

Selecting Objects

The first step to manipulating the objects on your PC is to select them—that is, mark them to indicate that they will be subject to some sort of user action.

Selecting a Single Object

This section demonstrates the technique for selecting a single object. As you practice, pay close attention to the changes that occur in the lists on the left side of the My Documents window.

① With My Documents open, click **My First Folder**; the My First Folder icon becomes shaded in blue, indicating that it is selected, and the File and Folder Tasks list expands with additional options.

② Double-click **My First Folder** to open it. "My Computer" is replaced by "My First Folder" in the window's title bar, and the contents of My First Folder are displayed.

 You'll learn more about opening objects later in this chapter, in the section "Opening Objects."

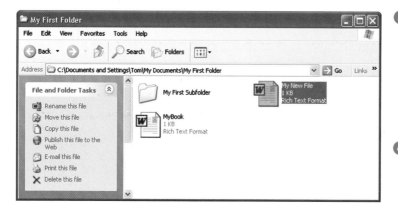

③ Click **My New File**. The My New File document becomes selected, and the File and Folder Tasks list changes, containing only those options that apply to files.

④ Click the **Back** button in the toolbar to return to the My Documents window.

Selecting Multiple Objects

There may be times when you need to perform the same action on several objects at once—perhaps to move numerous files from one folder to another. Rather than selecting each file and moving it one at a time, you can select every file that needs to be moved and perform a single move operation on all of them at once.

Depending on whether the files you need to select are adjacent or non-adjacent, you'll use a different technique to select them; these techniques are covered next.

Selecting Adjacent Objects

There are two ways to select adjacent objects: by using the "click and drag" technique or by pressing and holding down the SHIFT key while clicking objects with the mouse (this action is called "Shift-clicking").

To practice clicking and dragging to select multiple adjacent objects, do the following:

1. Place your mouse pointer in the top-left corner of the details pane in My Documents, above and to the left of the My eBooks folder.
2. Press and hold down the left mouse button, and drag the mouse pointer toward the bottom-right corner of My Documents. As you drag, a light blue box encloses the objects in the window; these objects become shaded in dark blue, indicating that they are selected.

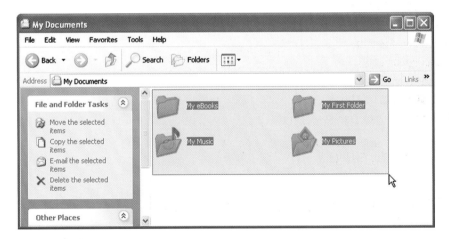

3. When you have selected all the objects in the My Documents window, release the left mouse button. The light blue box disappears, but the objects in the window remain selected.
4. Click a blank area in the My Documents window to deselect the objects. The objects return to their original, unshaded appearance.

To practice selecting multiple adjacent objects by Shift-clicking, do the following:

1 In the My Documents window, click the **My eBooks** folder to select it.

2 Press and hold down the **SHIFT** key on your keyboard.

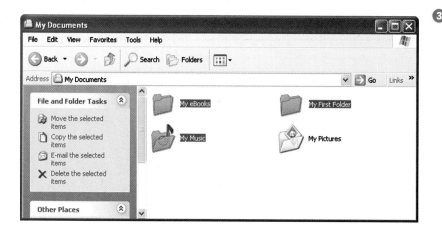

3 While holding down the SHIFT key, click the **My Music** folder in the My Documents window. The first three folders in the window, My eBooks, My First Folder, and My Music, are selected.

4 Click a blank area in the My Documents window to deselect the three folders.

Selecting Non-Adjacent Objects

To select multiple non-adjacent objects, press the **CTRL** key. Not surprisingly, this operation is referred to as Control-clicking. "Control-clicking" demands that you click each object you want to select. To get used to this technique, follow these steps:

1 In the My Documents window, click the **My eBooks** folder to select it.

2 Press and hold down the **CTRL** key on your keyboard.

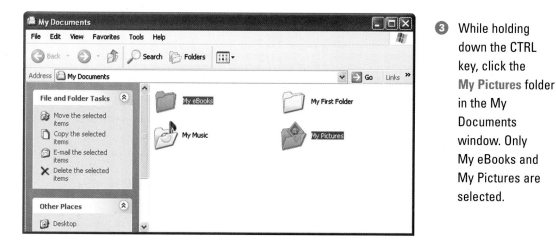

3 While holding down the CTRL key, click the **My Pictures** folder in the My Documents window. Only My eBooks and My Pictures are selected.

4 Click a blank area in the My Documents window to deselect the two folders.

Moving and Copying Objects

Now that you have learned how to select objects, you're ready to manipulate them. Some of the most common object-manipulation tasks are moving and copying objects from one location to another. For example, when you finish working on a file, you might decide to move it to a folder that contains projects you have completed.

When you move an object, it is placed in its new location and deleted from its original location. Copying an object, on the other hand, leaves the object intact in its original location and creates a duplicate object in the new location.

Moving Objects

Windows XP enables you to move and copy objects using a variety of techniques. For example, you can move objects using any of the following techniques:

- ✦ Drag and drop
- ✦ Cut and paste
- ✦ The Move this file task in the File and Folder Tasks list

To practice moving objects using drag and drop, do the following:

1 In My Documents, double-click **My First Folder**. The My First Folder window opens.

2 Click **My New File**. The My New File document is selected, and the File and Folder Tasks list expands to include additional tasks.

3 Click and hold your mouse button on **My New File** and drag the My New File icon to the My First Subfolder icon. My New File is moved from My First Folder to My First Subfolder.

4 Double-click **My First Subfolder**. The My First Subfolder window opens, displaying the My New File icon.

Although the drag-and-drop technique is a quick and easy way to move objects, it may not always be the most convenient—especially when the destination location is not displayed in the current window. In that case, you can use a cut-and-paste operation. Here's how:

1. In the My First Subfolder window, which you opened in the preceding steps, select the My New File icon.
2. Click the Edit menu and then click Cut. The My New File icon appears dimmed.
3. Click the Back button in the toolbar to return to the My First Folder window.
4. Click a blank area in the My First Folder window to ensure that no objects are selected.
5. Click the Edit menu bar and click Paste. My New File is moved from My First Subfolder to My First Folder.

More About... Edit Commands

You might have noticed some text to the right of the Cut, Copy, and Paste commands in the Edit menu. This text indicates the keyboard shortcut that can be used to execute each command instead of using Windows XP's menu system. For example, to perform a Cut operation, you can press CTRL+X—that is, simultaneously press the CTRL and X keys on your keyboard. Likewise, to perform a Paste operation, you can press CTRL+V, and to perform a Copy operation, you can press CTRL+C.

If you need to move an object from one location to another faraway location, such as to a different drive or to another computer on your network, you can use the Move this file task in the File and Folder Tasks list. That way, you don't have to waste time navigating your PC's organizational structure to locate the destination you need. Here's how:

1. In My First Folder, click MyBook. The File and Folder Tasks list expands to include a task named "Move this file."
2. Click Move this file. The Move Items dialog box opens.
3. In the Move Items dialog box, select the destination location for the object (in this case, Local Disk (C:)).
4. Click Move. The Move dialog box closes, and My New File is moved to the selected location.

Copying Objects

Just as there are several ways to move objects, there are several options when it comes to copying them:

+ CTRL drag and drop

+ Copy and paste

+ The Copy this file task in the File and Folder Tasks list

To learn how to copy objects using drag and drop, place a copy of My New File in My First Subfolder by doing the following:

1 With the My First Folder window open on your desktop, press and hold down the CTRL key.

2 With the CTRL key still pressed down, click and hold the My New File icon and drag it to My First Subfolder.

 As you CTRL drag and drop, watch the bottom-right corner of the mouse pointer. A plus sign should appear, indicating that a copy, not a move, is being performed.

3 Release the mouse button and CTRL key. Notice that the My New File icon still appears in the My First Folder window. Double-click My First Subfolder to open the My First Subfolder window.

4 After verifying that My First File is indeed in My First Subfolder, click the Back button in the toolbar to return to the My First Folder window.

If you want to copy an object to a destination that is not displayed in the current window, you can perform a copy-and-paste operation. Instead of using the Edit menu to issue these commands, however, this section demonstrates the use of shortcut menus to accomplish this task:

1 With the My First Folder window open on your desktop, right-click My New File, and then click Copy in the shortcut menu that appears.

2 Click the Back button to navigate to the My Documents folder.

3 Right-click a blank area in the My Documents window, and then click Paste in the shortcut menu that appears. A copy of My New File appears in the My Documents window.

4 Click the Forward button in the toolbar to return to the My First Folder window. Notice that this window still contains an icon for My New File.

Just as you can use the Move this file task to move an object from one location to another far away, such as a different drive or another computer on your network, you can use the Copy this file task to copy an object. Here's how:

1 In My First Folder, click My New File. The File and Folder Tasks list expands to include a task named "Copy this file."

2 Click Copy this file. The Copy Items dialog box opens.

3 In the Copy Items dialog box, select the destination location for the object (in this case, Local Disk (C:)).

4 Click Copy. The Copy dialog box closes, and My New File is copied to the selected location.

Deleting Objects

When you delete objects on your computer, you are temporarily placing them in the Recycle Bin. Doing so frees valuable disk space, and can help keep you organized. If you delete an object, but decide you did so in error, you can retrieve it from the Recycle Bin as long as the Recycle Bin hasn't been emptied (or until the Recycle Bin runs out of room and deletes it permanently).

Deleting objects is a relatively simple process, and there are several ways to accomplish the task. For example, you can use the menu system, a shortcut menu, or the DELETE key on your keyboard to delete objects. Alternatively, you can drag objects to the Recycle Bin icon on your desktop to delete them. This section steps you through the process of deleting files, folders, and shortcuts, as well as working with the Recycle Bin.

Deleting Files and Folders

Deleting files and folders are virtually the same; you have several deletion methods at your disposal. Deleted files and folders are placed in the Recycle Bin. Furthermore, folders need not be empty to be deleted. To learn how to delete files (deleting folders uses the same method), let's delete the files you moved and copied to the C: drive in the preceding section:

1 Click start and click My Computer.

2 Navigate to the Local Disk (C:) window.

3 In the Local Disk (C:) window, click MyBook to select it.

4 Click the File menu and click Delete. The Confirm File Delete dialog box opens.

5 Click Yes. A dialog box opens briefly to indicate the progress of the deletion. When the deletion is complete, you are returned to the Local Disk (C:) window, which no longer lists MyBook.

Confirm File Delete

Are you sure you want to send 'MyBook' to the Recycle Bin?

Yes   No

⑥ Click the **Close** button to close the Local Disk (C:) window and return to the desktop.

⑦ Click **start** and click **My Documents**. The My Documents window opens.

⑧ Double-click **My First Folder**. The My First Folder window opens.

⑨ Click **My New File** to select it.

⑩ Press the **DELETE** key on your keyboard. Once again, the Confirm File Delete dialog box opens.

⑪ Click **Yes**. As before, a dialog box opens briefly to indicate the progress of the deletion. When the deletion is complete, you are returned to the My First Folder window, which no longer lists My New File.

⑫ Click **My First Subfolder** and press the **DELETE** key on your keyboard to delete it.

⑬ Click **Yes** in the Confirm Folder Delete dialog box. The folder no longer exists in My First Folder.

Deleting Shortcuts

Are there shortcuts littering your desktop that you never use? One way to eliminate them is to simply delete them from your system. Doing so is simple: Just right-click the icon of the shortcut you want to delete and select **Delete** from the shortcut menu that appears. The shortcut is removed from the desktop.

To practice deleting shortcuts, do the following:

❶ Right-click the wordpad (2) shortcut on your desktop.

❷ Click **Delete** in the shortcut menu that appears.

❸ A Confirm File Delete dialog box appears. Click **Yes** to confirm deletion of the shortcut.

❹ The shortcut is deleted.

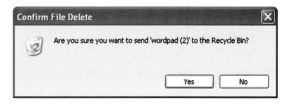

Deleting a shortcut does not delete the actual file.

Working with the Recycle Bin

If you realize you've deleted an object in error, you'll probably be able to recover it from the Recycle Bin. Sometimes the Recycle Bin has been emptied, has run out of room and deleted the object permanently, or files deleted using third-party software might not be placed in the Recycle Bin.

Restoring Deleted Items

The act of recovering objects from the Recycle Bin is called restoring; to restore objects, do the following:

 These steps assume the My First Folder window is still open on your desktop.

❶ Double-click the **Recycle Bin** icon in the lower-right corner of the desktop. The Recycle Bin window opens.

❷ In the Recycle Bin window, double-click **My First Subfolder**. The My First Subfolder Properties dialog box opens.

❸ Click the **Restore** button.

❹ Click **OK** to close the My First Subfolder Properties dialog box and restore the folder to its original location (that is, in My First Folder).

5. Arrange the Recycle Bin window and My First Folder window so that the Recycle Bin window is on top, but the contents of both are visible.

6. In the Recycle Bin window, click My New File to select it.

7. Click the File menu and click Restore. My New File is moved from the Recycle Bin window to the My First Folder window.

> Other ways to restore objects in the Recycle Bin include dragging them from the Recycle Bin window to the location where they belong, or right-clicking them in the Recycle Bin window and clicking Restore in the shortcut menu that appears.

Emptying the Recycle Bin

To free up hard-drive space in a pinch, you can empty the Recycle Bin. Here's how:

1. In the Recycle Bin window, click the File menu and click Empty Recycle Bin. The Confirm Multiple File Delete dialog box opens.

2. Click Yes. The Confirm Multiple File Delete dialog box closes, and the Recycle Bin is emptied.

3. Click the Close button to close the Recycle Bin window. Notice that the Recycle Bin desktop icon has changed to reflect the fact that the Recycle Bin is now empty.

Renaming Objects

As you know, an object is an entity, defined by a set of attributes. One of the most important attributes is an object's name. Although default names are supplied by Windows XP or the program being used to create the object, these names may not adequately describe the object. For example, when you create a file using WordPad, that file is named "Document" by default. Although this name describes the file's type, it doesn't indicate the file's contents. A better name for the WordPad file might be "Memoirs" or "Work Schedule" or "Great American Novel."

There are a few ways to rename objects: using the File menu, using shortcut menus, and so on. To learn how to rename objects, let's create a few new documents and rename them:

1 Click **start** and click **My Documents**. The My Documents window opens.

2 Right-click a blank space in the window. In the shortcut menu that appears, click **New**, and then click Text Document.

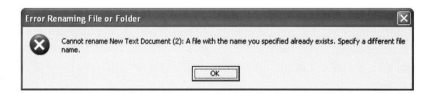

3 An icon for a new text document appears in the My Documents window; notice that its default name, "New Text Document," is selected. To accept the default name, press ENTER.

4 Repeat steps 2 and 3 to create a second document. Notice that this document's default name is "New Text Document (2)," making it unique in the folder.

5 Click **New Text Document** to select it.

6 Click the **File** menu and click **Rename**. The New Text Document name is selected.

7 Type **File1**, and press ENTER.

8 Right-click **New Text Document (2)** and click **Rename** in the shortcut menu that appears. The New Text Document (2) name is selected.

9 Type **File1**, and press ENTER. The Error Renaming File or Folder dialog box opens, indicating that you must specify another name for this file.

10 Click **OK**. The original name of the file is restored and is selected to be accepted or changed.

11 Type **File2**, and press **ENTER**. The file's name is changed.

 To rename a desktop shortcut, right-click it and click **Rename** in the shortcut menu that appears. The shortcut's name is selected; type the name you want, and press **ENTER**.

Opening Objects

You can open any object accessible through My Computer or the Windows Explorer by right-clicking it and choosing Open from the shortcut menu that appears. Selecting this command starts whatever application is associated with the object and displays that object's contents in a window for you to view—or for further work, if you're so inclined.

You can use this technique to access or edit the objects you've worked with in previous sections. Here's how:

1 In the My Documents window, right-click **File1** (created in the preceding section) and click **Open** in the shortcut menu that appears.

2 Notepad starts with File1 open in the workspace for your inspection or further work.

3 Click the **Close** button to close Notepad.

4 Click the **Close** button to close My Documents.

If you try this technique on an object that Windows XP doesn't recognize—for example, a file named File1.xyz, Windows XP displays a dialog box indicating that it doesn't know what program to use to open the object.

```
┌─────────────────────────────────────────────────────────┐
│ Windows                                          [?][X]   │
├─────────────────────────────────────────────────────────┤
│  ┌──┐   Windows cannot open this file:                    │
│  │  │                                                      │
│  └──┘   File:   File1.xyz                                  │
│                                                            │
│  To open this file, Windows needs to know what program    │
│  created it.  Windows can go online to look it up          │
│  automatically, or you can manually select from a list of  │
│  programs on your computer.                                │
│                                                            │
│  What do you want to do?                                   │
│   ⊙ Use the Web service to find the appropriate program    │
│   ○ Select the program from a list                         │
│                                                            │
│                            ┌────────┐  ┌────────┐          │
│                            │   OK   │  │ Cancel │          │
│                            └────────┘  └────────┘          │
└─────────────────────────────────────────────────────────┘
```

8

This dialog box gives you two options:

✦ **Use the Web service to find the appropriate program.** Click **OK** to search Microsoft's File Associations database on the Web to determine whether a program is known to be associated with files of type xyz. Results of the search appear in a Web browser window. You must have a working Internet connection for this to work. If no match is found, you'll see a display like the one shown here.

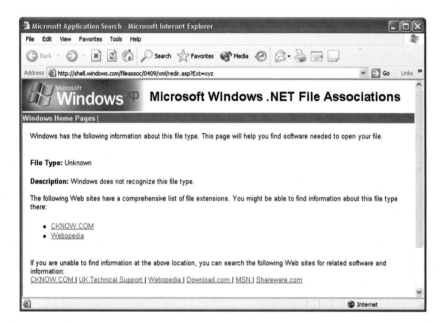

✦ **Select the program from a list.** To specify which program should be used to open the file, click the **Select the program from a list** option button and click **OK.** The Open With dialog box opens; from here, you can select any program already installed on your PC (you can use NotePad or WordPad for mystery files, just to see what they contain).

Using the Search Companion

Programs, documents, and other files sometimes get buried quite deep in the folder structure of your hard drive. To work efficiently you should know how to find files on your computer. You can use Windows XP's Search Companion feature to sniff out just about any object, no matter where it is, using all kinds of different attributes to help narrow or qualify your searches.

For example, when searching for a file or folder, the Search Companion lets you specify the following kinds of information to help narrow your searches:

- ◆ **File name.** Enter complete or partial file names to look for specific files by name.

- ◆ **Text contents.** Specify text that must occur within a file for it to be selected during a search.

- ◆ **Location.** Specify search targets, from individual containers (default folders like My Documents or drives on your PC) to My Computer (to search every accessible location on your PC).

Other search options enable you to further narrow your search, including restrictions on file dates, file types (such as word processing, spreadsheet, picture, music, or video files), file sizes, and other controls. In addition to enabling you to search for objects on your own PC, Search Companion also allows you to search for computers on your network, if applicable, people in your address book, and information in the Help and Support Center. You can even use Search Companion to search for information on the Internet (if an Internet connection exists).

8

The following steps show you how to launch and use the Windows Search Companion:

1 Click the start button, then on the right panel, click Search. The Search Results window opens. On the left side of the Search Results window, you'll find the Search Companion, an animated character, and a list of search options, as shown in Figure 8-2.

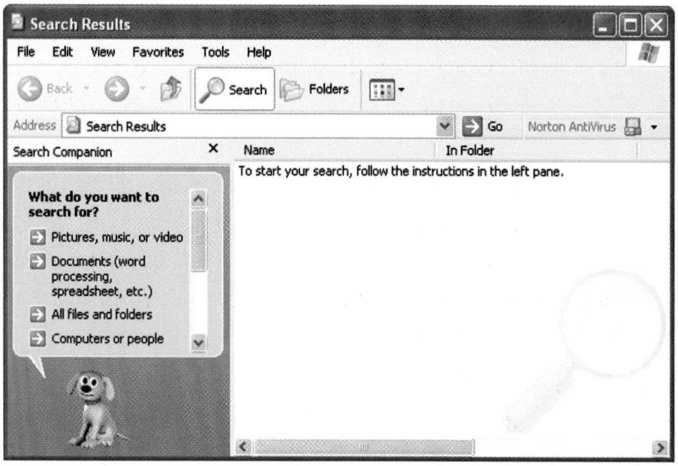

Figure 8-2 Use the Search Companion to locate files, folders, computers, or other data.

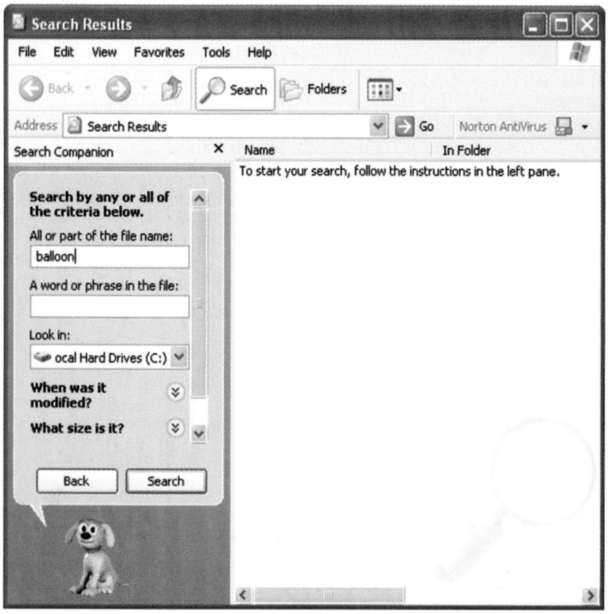

2 Click the type of file you want to locate. A list of search criteria will appear. The choices that appear depend on the type of file you are searching for.

3. If you are looking for a file or folder, type any or all of the file name or folder name, or click in the **A word or phrase in the file** text box and type the requested word or phrase. This tells the Search Companion to look beyond the file name into the actual documents.

 If you type multiple words in either text box, Windows will find all files that have any of those words in the file name or contents.

You have the option of specifying where to look for the text. You can search any specific disk drive or the entire computer.

4. Click the down arrow next to the Look in list box, and then select a drive or folder. If you want to search all your available drives, (including network drives), choose **My Computer**.

5. Click **Search**. The search will begin.

Windows will display the results of the search on the right side of the window. The name of the file is listed as well as its folder location, size, type, and the date it was last modified. You can double-click a file to open it in the application it was created.

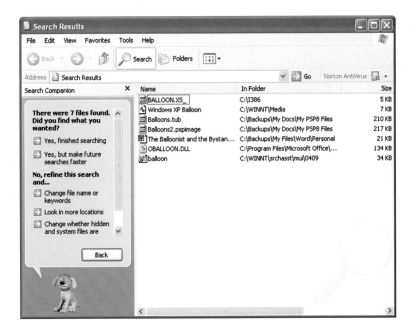

CHAPTER **9**

Explore the Use of CDs/DVDs

One of the reasons people use their computer is for multimedia activities, such as playing music and movies. Understanding how to use CDs and DVDs, where much of this multimedia content originates, is essential to getting the most out of your PC. In this chapter, you'll discover how to use the CD and DVD drives and be introduced to various types of CD and DVD media. You'll even explore a few popular media playback tools. Finally, you'll learn how to use CDs and DVDs to install new software on your computer. By the time you finish this chapter, your PC's multimedia features will no longer be a mystery.

Utilizing CD/DVD Drives and Media

Your PC allows you to play back CDs and/or DVDs, just as you do using your stereo and home theater. However, your PC may also give you the added advantage of being able to burn your own CDs and DVDs.

A CD can contain music, data, or both. Some audio CDs include multimedia files (audio, video, animation, movies, software, etc.) that go along with the music, while data CDs typically contain data files, multimedia files, or software. For example, many software programs—including Windows XP—come on data CDs, from which they can be installed. A DVD, on the other hand, can contain a movie, data, or both. As with data CDs, DVDs can be used to store data files, multimedia files, and software. Unlike CDs, however, which max out at between 650 and 700 MB of data, DVDs can hold as much as 17 GB of data.

 Data CDs and DVDs can also contain music files, but these differ from the types found on audio CDs. Music files require PC software for playback, while audio CDs can be played in a typical CD player.

The discs you place in a CD/DVD drive are typically referred to as media. You'll need to pay close attention to the type of media you use to ensure it supports the task you want to perform. For example, if you want to burn a DVD, you'll need to make sure you're using a DVD-R or DVD-RAM and not a DVD-ROM. Also, make sure your drive can read that media type—you won't be able to burn a DVD in a CD-ROM drive. Because many CDs and DVDs are exactly the same size and color (see Figure 9-1), you might not be able to identify a disc's media type simply by looking at it. If the media type is not printed on the disc itself, look at the original packaging to determine whether the disc is a CD-ROM, CD-R, CD-RW, DVD-ROM, DVD-R, or DVD-RAM.

As mentioned in Chapter 1, there are three types of CD drives and three types of DVD drives:

Figure 9-1 CD/DVD media.

✦ **CD-ROM drive.** A CD-ROM drive reads information on CD-ROMs. CD-ROMs can be read, but not written to.

✦ **CD-R drive.** A CD-R drive can read information on CD-ROMs and write information to CD-Rs. A CD-R can be written to, or burned, only once.

✦ **CD-RW drive.** A CD-RW drive can read information on CD-ROMs and write information to CD Rs and CD-RWs. A CD-RW is a CD that you can write to several times.

✦ **DVD drive.** A DVD drive reads information on DVD-ROMs. Like CD-ROMs, DVD-ROMs can be read, but not written to.

✦ **DVD-R drive.** A DVD-R drive can read information on DVD-ROMs and write information to DVD-Rs. A DVD-R can be written to, or burned, only once.

✦ **DVD-RAM drive.** A DVD-RAM drive can read information on DVD-ROMs and write information to DVD-Rs and DVD-RAMs. A DVD-RAM is a DVD that you can write to many times.

Your computer might have a drive that plays CDs, burns CD-Rs or CD-RWs, plays DVDs, or burns DVD-Rs or DVD-RAMs. Many CD/DVD drives are combination players. For example, some CD-RW drives can also play DVDs.

You need to know what kinds of CD or DVD drives your PC has because that determines what types of media your computer can read. If you have a plain CD-ROM drive, you can read CDs, but you can't burn your own CDs or play DVDs. If you have a

9

DVD drive, you can play CDs, but cannot burn CD-Rs or CD-RWs. Table 9-1 lists uses for each type of CD or DVD drive.

Table 9-1 Types of CD/DVD drives and their uses.

TASK	CD-ROM	CD-R	CD-RW	DVD	DVD-R	DVD-RAM
Play CDs	✔	✔	✔	✔	✔	✔
Read data CDs	✔	✔	✔	✔	✔	✔
Burn CD-Rs		✔	✔			✔
Burn CD-RWs			✔			✔
Play DVDs				✔	✔	✔
Read data DVDs				✔	✔	✔
Burn DVD-Rs					✔	✔
Burn DVD-RAMs						✔

Using Your CD/DVD Drive

No matter what type of media you plan to use in your CD/DVD drive, the procedure is essentially the same. Only a few simple steps are required. Before you use your drive, however, there are a few precautions you should take:

✦ Always use the button on the CD/DVD drive to open and close the drawer. Never force the drawer in or out.

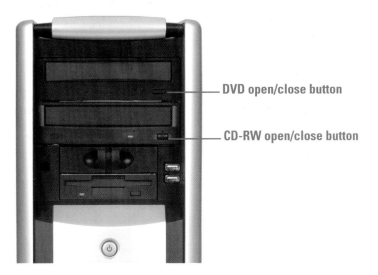

DVD open/close button

CD-RW open/close button

Some multimedia programs include an Eject button or command you can use to open the CD/DVD drive drawer.

✦ Make sure the CD/DVD media you place in the CD/DVD drive drawer is centered within the grooves, notches, or depression in the drawer.

✦ Never place anything other than CD/DVD media in or on your CD/DVD drive drawer. Doing so could damage the drive.

✦ Always place CD/DVD media with its label face up.

✦ Always hold CD/DVD media by the edges or stick your finger in the center hole. Fingerprints and smudges on the data side of the CD/DVD media might cause skipping or prevent reading or writing.

To use your CD/DVD drive, follow these steps:

1 Press the open/close button on the front of your CD/DVD drive. The CD/DVD drive drawer opens.

2 Pick up the CD/DVD media by its edges only or by placing a finger in the center hole.

3 Place the CD/DVD media in the tray with the label facing up. Move the media into the center of the drawer so that it fits within the defined holding area.

4 Press the open/close button on the front of your CD/DVD drive. The CD/DVD drive drawer closes.

The PC scans the CD/DVD disc to see what type of media it is. Depending on the speed of your drive, this may take a few moments.

9

Playing Audio CDs

The first time you insert a CD or DVD into your PC, Windows XP displays a dialog box asking you what you want to do next. For example, if you insert an audio CD, Windows XP displays the Audio CD dialog box, shown in Figure 9-2.

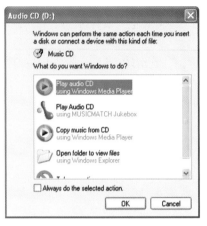

Figure 9-2 The Audio CD dialog box.

The default CD player may vary from machine to machine. Windows Media Player is a common one, but your machine might use a different program to play CDs, such as MusicMatch® Jukebox. If your PC uses a different CD player, read its user manual or open the help menu on the program's menu bar to learn how to operate it.

This dialog box lists four options:

Figure 9-3 The Windows Media Player.

✦ **Play Audio CD.** Select this option to play the audio CD using the default player (in this case, Windows Media Player, shown in Figure 9-3).

✦ **Copy music from CD.** Use this option to launch the Windows Media Player and begin the process to copy selected songs to your computer hard drive.

✦ **Open folder to view files.** This option is used to view the files on the disc in a Windows Explorer window (see Figure 9-4).

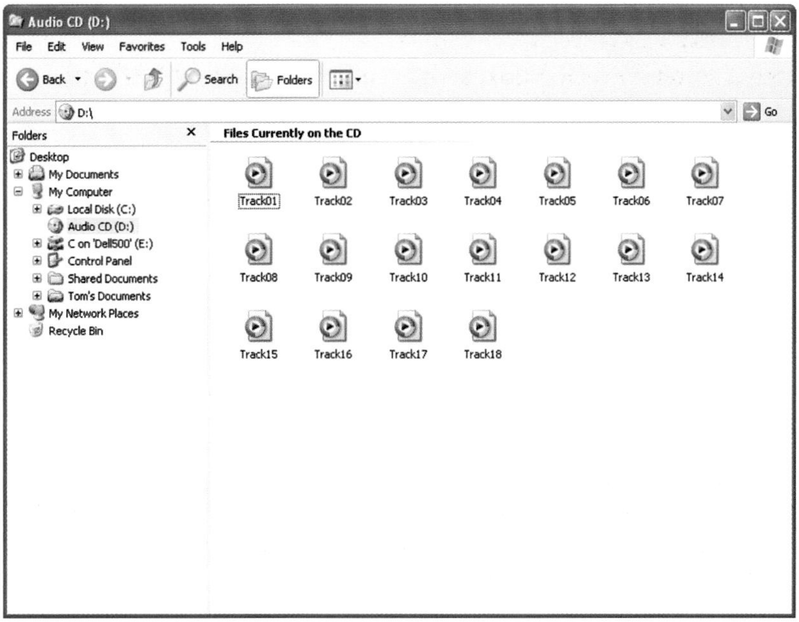

Figure 9-4 Windows Explorer window with audio track file icons.

✦ **Take no action.** When choosing this option, the dialog box will close and no action is taken on the CD.

Select the action you want to perform on the audio CD. If you know that you'll want to take the same action each time you insert an audio CD into your PC, check the **Always do the selected action** check box at the bottom of the dialog box, and then click **OK**. That way, the next time you insert an audio CD into the CD drive, Windows will automatically play back the CD without displaying the Audio CD dialog box first.

> If you select the **Always do the selected action** check box for one type of media, such as an audio CD, it applies only to that type of media. If you insert a different type of media into the drive, such as a DVD-ROM, Windows XP will display a dialog box similar to the one for audio CDs, asking you what action you want to take. Make your selection just as you did for audio CDs.

Using Windows Media Player

You can use Windows Media Player (see Figure 9-5) to play audio CDs, music files, and video files, as well as to access Internet radio, television, and movie programs. You can even use Windows Media Player to copy music from CDs to your hard drive, create custom playlists, burn new audio CDs, and transfer music files to portable audio players.

Figure 9-5 The Windows Media Player.

The controls built into Windows Media Player for listening to audio CDs are similar to those on your portable, car, or home CD player. Table 9-2 lists the common controls in a typical Windows-based CD player.

Table 9-2 The common CD player controls.

USE THIS BUTTON	TO
Play	Start the music. Once the CD is playing, the Play button becomes the Pause button.
Pause	Pause the music. To restart the music, click the Play/Pause button.
Stop	Stop the music.
Back	Skip to the previous song.
Forward	Skip to the next song.
Mute	Turn off the sound.
Volume	Change the volume. Drag the slider bar up or down to adjust volume levels.
Time	Move ahead or back within a song. Drag the slider bar to jump to a specific spot.

> **More About . . . Controlling Audio Players**
>
> Most programs, including Windows Media Player, can be controlled through mouse actions or keyboard shortcuts. To learn exactly what keystrokes you can use to control Windows Media Player, click the **Help** menu, and then click **Help Topics**. You can find a list of keyboard shortcuts by searching for the word shortcuts.

To use Windows Media Player to play CDs, do the following:

1. Insert the CD you want to listen to in your CD/DVD drive.
2. If Windows Media Player does not start automatically, click the **start** button, point to **All Programs**, and click **Windows Media Player** (or click the **Windows Media Player** icon on the left side of the start menu).

 If a program other than Windows Media Player starts when you insert the CD, simply click the program window's **Close** button to close the program.

3. Click **Play** to start the music.

9

In addition to these common playback buttons, the Windows Media Player window has the same controls as any other program window, including Minimize and Close. The normal rectangular workspace area, however, is hidden. Click the **Show menu bar** button to reveal this area.

Show menu bar button

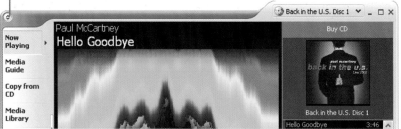

When you are finished listening to your CD, click the **Close** button to exit Windows Media Player. You can leave your audio CD in the CD/DVD drive or remove it. To remove the media from the drive, do the following:

1 Press the open/close button on the front of your CD/DVD drive. The drive drawer opens.

2 Pick up the CD by its edges or by placing a finger in the center hole, and remove it from the tray.

3 Press the open/close button on the front of your drive. The drive drawer closes.

> ### More About . . . Using MusicMatch Jukebox
>
> Another popular media player is the MusicMatch Jukebox. MusicMatch Jukebox is similar in nature to Windows Media Player. They have similar controls, such as volume control, play, pause, stop, mute, forward, and back buttons.

Playing DVDs

Playing DVD movies is almost as easy as playing an audio CD, but you may need to install a DVD compression and encryption decoder driver first.

Some DVD movies include a playback tool. In that case, you can simply play the DVD using this simple tool.

One easy way to get the driver you need is to purchase and install a third-party DVD player program, such as WinDVD from InterVideo or PowerDVD from CyberLink. In doing so, you'll install the compression and encryption decoder driver needed to play DVDs.

Alternatively, if you bought your PC from a large computer company, such as Gateway, it most likely came pre-installed with a DVD player program of some kind. Additionally, many DVDs themselves include the PCFriendly DVD player (see Figure 9-6). If you don't already have a DVD player installed, select to install the DVD player from the DVD media when prompted.

Figure 9-6 The WinDVD player.

Once you have a DVD compression and encryption decoder installed, you can use a third-party DVD player or Windows Media Player to play your movies. Most third-party DVD players have simple controls, including play, pause, stop, fast forward, skip forward, rewind, and skip backward. If you aren't sure how to use your specific third-party player, consult its user guide or the software's help menu.

To use Windows Media Player to play a DVD movie, do the following:

❶ Insert the DVD media into the DVD drive.

❷ If any program windows or dialog boxes open other than Windows Media Player, click the **Close** button to exit them.

❸ Click **start**, point to **All Programs**, and then click **Windows Media Player** (or click **Windows Media Player** on the left side of the start menu). The Windows Media Player window opens.

9

④ In the left column of buttons, click **Now Playing**.

⑤ Click the drop-down arrow in the upper-right corner, and select the DVD drive.

⑥ Once the DVD drive is selected, Windows Media Player should play the DVD automatically. If it doesn't, click the **Play** button.

⑦ To view the movie in full-screen mode, click the **View Full Screen** button located in the lower-right corner below the video image. The movie is resized to the maximum size possible for your screen. Windows Media Player controls appear as tabs at the top and bottom of your screen; after a few seconds, these disappear.

 To regain access to the Windows Media Player controls during movie playback, simply move the mouse. If the controls don't reappear immediately, click the mouse near the bottom of the screen.

⑧ Navigate the DVD control menu using the mouse. Just point and click to the option of your choice, such as playing the movie, changing audio settings, viewing scene outlines, or accessing the bonus material on the DVD.

⑨ When you finish watching the DVD movie, click the **Close** button in the Windows Media Player window.

⑩ Remove the DVD media from the DVD drive, as described in the section "Using Windows Media Player."

Installing Software from a CD or DVD

Because CDs enable a software company to include as much as 700 MB of files on a single disc, software is often distributed on CDs. To store the same amount of data that fits on a single CD, you'd need 487 floppies!

 Recently, manufacturers began distributing their software on DVDs, which can hold a whopping 17 GB of data—equivalent to 6,250 floppy disks!

Most software products use less than half a CD's capacity, even when lots of extras and bonuses are included. A few software products and several games, however, do come on multiple CDs or on a single DVD disc.

9

Although you install and load programs from a CD and a DVD the same basic way, the specific steps of an installation process will vary by program. For this reason, it's wise to read the program's installation manual and user guide before inserting CD/DVD media into your PC. Then, follow these general steps to install software from a CD/DVD (remember, you must be logged on to a computer administrator user account to install programs):

 If the steps in your software CD/DVD's user manual differ from the ones shown here, follow the ones in the user manual.

1 Close any programs that are currently open on your PC, including your anti-virus software.
2 Insert the CD/DVD into the appropriate drive.
3 If this is the first time the program CD/DVD has been inserted into your PC, Windows XP will look for a special file called autorun; if it finds this file, the operating system then executes its instructions. Typically, a Welcome screen with the company and product name appears; look for a **Next**, **Continue**, or **OK** button on the screen, and click it.

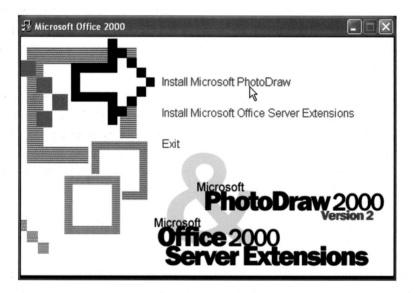

4 You should see a list of options; look for one labeled "Install" or "Setup." When you find it, click it.

 Most software CD/DVDs, in addition to offering an install option, include other options, such as view samples, watch demos, work through a tutorial, see advertisements, or read documentation.

5 Follow any additional on-screen prompts.

 In most cases, you can accept default selections on any subsequent setup screen. However, it's always a good idea to review the installation manual before initiating an install.

If no Welcome screen appears when you insert the CD or DVD, follow these steps:

1. Click the **start** button, and then click **My Computer** to open My Computer.
2. Double-click the CD or DVD drive icon.
3. In the top level of the CD or DVD drive, look for a Setup or Install program icon. When you find it, double-click it.

 If you don't see a Setup or Install icon, consult the software's user manual for details on how to install the product.

4. Follow the on-screen prompts or the steps in the installation user guide.

During the course of installing a software product, you'll often be prompted to perform several common activities, including:

✦ **Agree to a user license.** This typically requires you to read a lengthy legal document and click the **I Agree** button to proceed with the installation.

✦ **Provide a product key.** A product key is a string of letters and/or numbers that uniquely identifies a product you've purchased; these are used to prevent software piracy. Without a product key, most software will not install or function properly. You can usually find the product key on your software packaging.

✦ **Indicate an install path.** An install path is a folder on a local hard drive where the bulk of the software product will be installed. In most cases, you'll want to install the program in C:\Program Files\product name, where product name is the exact or representational name of the software product. The setup routine usually suggests a location; it's a good practice to stick with the suggested location.

✦ **Restart.** Some programs require you to restart your system to complete the installation process.

Once your software is installed, an icon for the product should appear in the start menu, on the desktop, or both. To start the program, click the software's icon in the All Programs menu, or double-click the software's desktop icon.

9

Surf the Web and Stay in Touch with E-mail

As you begin to explore the Internet, you'll want to take advantage of its fascinating features, including access to innumerable Web sites containing vast amounts of information. Many Web sites not only include informative text, but also pictures, video, and audio clips. You can discover how to "open the doors" to safe and secure online shopping whether you just want to buy a book from an online bookstore or buy a fabulous antique through an online auction. Finally, you can enjoy your leisure time playing your favorite games with someone on the other side of the world or chatting with family and friends online. This chapter explores the kinds of things you can do online—from the mundane to the marvelous.

Discovering the Online World

Most people have heard of the Internet, even if they don't really know what it is or what it can offer them. Simply put, the Internet is a global network of computers designed to share information and support communications. There are more than 150 million computers already on the Internet, and more are added daily. When you go online, you are connecting your computer to this vast network, and in turn, you can access the Internet's vast information resources. The Internet is a virtual worldwide library that grows larger everyday! The information you view on your computer screen might be stored on a computer in Athens, Georgia or Athens, Greece. When you are on the Internet, everything in the online world is right at your fingertips, a constantly changing treasure chest ready for you to explore.

However, the Internet is more than a repository of data. The online world has much to offer those who want to explore it. Using the Internet, you can:

✦ Send and receive mail (called e-mail, short for electronic mail)

✦ Read books, magazines, and newspaper articles

✦ Shop for products

✦ Check the weather and local news

✦ Read product reviews and evaluations

✦ Catch the latest sports scores

✦ Make airline, hotel, and car-rental reservations

- ✦ Participate in multiplayer games

- ✦ Download computer programs, pictures, and music

- ✦ Attend live concerts, sporting events, plays, or other special events

- ✦ Communicate with others via audio/video conferencing

- ✦ Chat with others in "real time"

- ✦ Research family history, find long-lost friends or schoolmates

- ✦ And much more!

The Internet by itself is not the entire online world. There are numerous other communities online. The America Online® Service is an example of an online service you may recognize. In the same vein, the World Wide Web is not the whole Internet, either. The Web may get most of the attention and visibility, but it's just one of the many services and resources that the Internet offers.

Understanding Internet Terminology

Before you eagerly dive into the online world, you should become familiar with some of the Internet's unique terminology. As mentioned previously, the Internet is a global network of computers. A network is two or more computers connected by a communication medium, such as a cable and network interface card (NIC), so that they can exchange files and other data.

An Internet service provider (ISP) or online service is a company that sells access to the Internet. ISPs typically offer Internet access and other services such as e-mail, while online services also offer their members specialized information and services. Your PC dials up or connects to the ISP or online service, which then connects you to the Internet.

A large part of the Internet is the World Wide Web, often called the Web for short. The Web is a vast collection of interconnected information that is displayed or presented in both graphical and textual form. Some of this information comes from schools, companies, governments, and professional groups, whereas other information comes from individuals just like you.

To access the Web, you typically use a software utility called a Web browser—also called a browser for short. If your PC is running Windows XP, you already have a browser—

10

Internet Explorer, as shown in Figure 10-1. Microsoft's Internet Explorer is one of the most widely used browsers on the Internet. You can also use other browsers, such as Netscape Navigator® and Opera. To make things easier for you, some ISPs and online services offer a customized browser designed to grant you access to exclusive content and specialized features.

Figure 10-1 Internet Explorer, a Web browser.

Web browsers let you view Web sites. A Web site is a collection of online documents, maintained by a group or an individual, that addresses one or more topics. A Web site might contain information about someone's cat, a new bicycle model, a new product, a business, or almost anything else you could imagine. Many Web sites offer downloadable programs and products for you to purchase. Web sites can include pictures, sounds, and even animation and video clips.

A Web site is made up of one or more Web pages, formatted for viewing in your Web browser. A Web page is like a page in a book—a container for text and other content. A Web page usually includes links to other Web pages or Web sites. Figure 10-1 not only depicts Internet Explorer in use as a Web browser, it also displays a specific Web page about Gateway, Inc.

Hyperlinks or links are text or graphics on a Web page that you can click to go to another Web page or to download a file (such as a program, music file, or picture). Text links appear in a different color than surrounding text and often are underlined. Graphics are usually only indicated by positioning your mouse pointer over a graphical element to see if the pointer changes from an arrow to a hand with a pointing finger.

 When you move your mouse pointer over any link, the pointer changes from an arrow to a hand with a pointing finger.

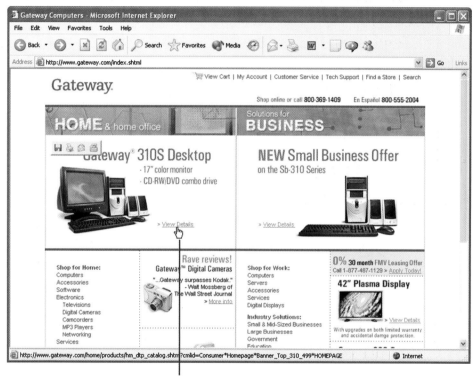

Mouse pointer

A home page is a predefined Web page that your Web browser loads each time it starts. It is common to set your home page to display local news, local weather, or something else of personal interest. For example, many companies set their employees' Web browsers to open to the main page of the company Web site.

Every site on the Internet has an address called a uniform resource locator (URL), a string of characters containing all the information needed to connect to a particular Web page. Here are some sample URLs:

10

- ✦ http://www.gateway.com
- ✦ http://www.ebay.com
- ✦ http://www.microsoft.com
- ✦ http://www.amazon.com

A Web server is a computer on the Internet that houses one or more Web sites. Web browsers communicate with Web servers to access Web pages. The browser manages the transfer of elements (text, graphics, etc.) to produce the Web page you see on your monitor.

E-mail describes a number of messaging systems used on the Internet and online services. E-mail messages are usually just text, but can include pictures, formatting, and animation. You can also attach just about any kind of file to an e-mail message. To use e-mail, you need a piece of software called an e-mail client, which is a program that's used to read and send messages.

 If your PC runs Windows XP, you already have an e-mail client—namely Outlook Express.

In addition to e-mail software, you also need an e-mail account with an associated e-mail address in order to send and receive e-mail. An e-mail account is a service you get from an ISP, online service, or an independent Internet company, such as Yahoo or Hotmail. An e-mail address is a unique address other people use to send you messages. All e-mail addresses are comprised of a person's name, nickname, or other identifier and the name of an ISP, online service, or company, separated by the @ sign. For example, **christine.smith@spotshop.com** is an e-mail address.

Surfing the Web

A Web browser is an essential tool for anyone using the Internet or other online services. Without a browser, it's impossible to access the vast amounts of information online. Fortunately, numerous browsers are available for your PC. As mentioned previously, if your PC is running Windows XP, you already have a browser—Internet Explorer.

Although every browser has some unique features and capabilities, most share common basic controls for browsing Web pages. Because we know you already have Internet Explorer on your PC, we'll use it as our example and teaching tool in this chapter. After you learn how to use Internet Explorer, you can apply that knowledge to any other browser you might run into.

Let's take a look at the basic Internet Explorer program window. As shown in Figure 10-2, an Internet Explorer window includes all the common program-window controls, in addition to standard browser controls within Internet Explorer. In addition to button controls, Web browsers offer multiple menu commands.

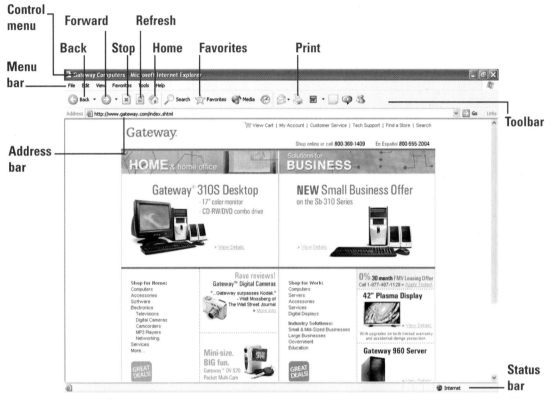

Figure 10-2 A maximized Internet Explorer program window.

Common browser controls include the following:

The buttons that appear in a browser's toolbars to represent these controls may differ, but their functions are always the same. The icons shown here are from Internet Explorer 6.0 as it appears in Windows XP.

✦ **Address bar.** The Address bar displays a URL for the Web page currently on display in the browser. To jump directly to another Web site, you can click the **Address bar**, type in the URL to replace what's displayed, and then press **ENTER** or click **Go**.

10

- **Back button.** Click the **Back** button once to jump to the Web page viewed prior to the page currently on display, or repeatedly to re-visit pages from even earlier in your Web session. In many browsers, the Back button features a small downward-pointing arrow, which you can click to display a list of as many as 10 recently visited pages. To jump to a page in the list, simply click it.

 If you just opened the browser, the Back button is inactive since no previously visited Web pages to return to exist.

- **Forward button.** If you've clicked the Back button at least once, the Forward button becomes active. Click it to return to the page you were viewing when you clicked the Back button. Like the Back button, the Forward button in most browsers maintains a drop-down list of recently visited pages.

- **Stop button.** Click the **Stop** button to terminate the loading of any Web page. For example, if a Web page contains a large graphic, it may take longer to load, so clicking the Stop button halts the loading of the Web page but displays all Web page elements that have arrived successfully.

- **Refresh button.** Click the **Refresh** button to reload the most updated version of the current Web page. This is useful in the event a page hasn't loaded correctly or if it's a page that changes frequently, such as a stock-ticker page or one that's tracking a live sports event.

- **Home button.** Click the **Home** button to load your home page, the page loaded by default when the Web browser is first opened. The Home button offers a convenient way to get to your home page without clicking the Back button repeatedly.

- **Print button.** Click the **Print** button to print the information currently displayed on the Web page. You can also choose File, Print from the menu bar.

- **Favorites, Add to Favorites.** Click the **Favorites** button to save the location of the current Web page in your Favorites list. Internet Explorer uses "Favorites." Other browsers, such as Netscape Navigator, use "Bookmarks" to mean the same thing.

If you want to save the information you see, printing is a good way to capture a Web page's contents. You should note, however, that some Web pages occupy multiple pages when printed, and that some graphical elements (especially animation and video) may not print exactly as they appear on screen.

Shopping Online

Where there's money to be made, the entrepreneurs won't be far behind. Literally thousands of online retail stores have set up shop over the past five years or so, making shopping one of the most popular activities on the Internet. It's so popular that many

brick-and-mortar stores (i.e., those buildings where you can go to shop) are finding that online shopping is creating significant competition. Today you can purchase almost anything—including groceries, clothing, books, housewares, cars, and electronics—online.

People have discovered that they can get what they want online in a fraction of the time it takes to shop in brick-and-mortar stores. They don't have to deal with traffic, crowds, or salespeople; they can have their purchases delivered to their door; and they can do it all while wearing their pajamas! The old saying "shop 'til you drop" doesn't really apply to Internet shopping.

How to Shop Online

Shopping online is usually a simple process. In most cases, the hardest part is finding the store you want. But once you're at an online store, what should you do?

Although each online store has unique features and layout, they almost all have a few common elements:

✦ A catalog or list of their products

✦ A search tool to find products

✦ A virtual shopping cart

✦ A virtual checkout

Figure 10-3 shows Amazon.com®, which is a very well-known online store.

Virtual shopping cart

Catalog browsing

Search tool

Catalog browsing

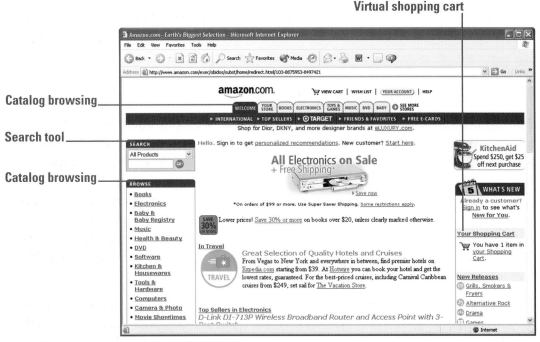

Figure 10-3 The Amazon.com home page.

From the home page of an online store, you usually have two options. You can either browse through its entire inventory or use a search tool to find what you want. If you already know exactly what you want, search tools are usually the best way to go. You only need to type the name of the item, and if the retailer sells it, you'll be quickly taken to it.

If you need to look around or "browse" for ideas and get a sense of what the online store is like, check out its online catalog. An online catalog is usually a collection of the products sold by the store, with pictures, descriptions, and prices of the items. Online catalogs may be arranged alphabetically, by product code, by manufacturer, by category, by price, or by a myriad of other possible organizational schemes.

To view an online store's catalog, look for links that include obvious words such as products, browse, catalog, index, inventory, and so on.

Credit Card Safety

Many people won't shop online because they fear credit card theft or the unauthorized use of a credit card to make a purchase. Ironically, more credit card thefts happen in person than online. Yes, there have been well-publicized occurrences of online credit theft, but they are few and far between.

This isn't to say that online credit card theft doesn't take place. Rather, the media heavily publicizes the few thefts that do occur. Making purchases online with a credit card can be more secure than making a purchase at a brick-and-mortar establishment.

Online Security

Online purchases are more secure for several reasons. Reputable online stores use sophisticated security mechanisms to protect your credit card and contact information. Basically, this security mechanism encrypts, or encodes, the information sent between your Web browser and the online retailer's Web server. This mechanism is known as SSL (Secure Sockets Layer), but how it actually works isn't important. What is important is that SSL-protected Web communications are especially difficult to access. When you submit your credit card information to an online store, your data is sent quickly, so it's unlikely that anyone will be able intercept it, and even if it were intercepted, it would take years to break the security code to extract the contents.

In addition to protecting the communication between your Web browser and their Web servers, reputable online stores also have an encrypted and protected database in which your information is stored. Most stores don't retain your credit card information any longer than necessary to process your order, charge your card, and verify that they have received the money for your purchase. Once that transaction is completed, most online stores delete your credit card information from their database.

 Some online retailers offer the option of storing your credit card information, simplifying the steps you need to take the next time you place an order with them. It's up to you whether to take advantage of this option.

Improve Online Credit Card Security

You can take a few precautionary actions to even further improve the security of your credit cards online.

You can decline the opportunity to store your credit card information with the company for future use. Although these stores usually employ additional security precautions to ensure that their credit card information database is fully protected, if you're at all nervous about storing your information with the company, don't do it. Simply elect not to save your data when the Web site offers.

Online retailers have joined with credit card companies to make Web shopping safer than making purchases in brick-and-mortar stores. Most credit card companies offer online purchase protection. Online purchase protection is a benefit that allows you to dispute a

10

charge on your credit card from any online store. If a purchase you didn't make appears on your statement, the credit card company will remove the charge with no hassle.

> **More About . . . Credit Card Security**
>
> Many credit card companies track your spending habits. If they notice that your credit card is being used to make purchases at stores you've never purchased from before or if the cost of purchases is significantly larger than the cost of your average purchase, they will automatically suspend your account. In most cases, your credit card company will contact you immediately to ask whether you made the suspect charges.

Here are a few other tips to ensure that you use your credit card wisely when shopping online:

✦ Always choose reputable stores.

✦ Keep track of all purchases made with your credit card so you can pinpoint charges on your statement that shouldn't be there.

✦ When in doubt about an online store's security, call the store directly to place an order (most offer their phone numbers on their order page or on their contact page).

 If you have multiple credit cards, you can even designate one to use solely for online purchases.

The Benefits of Shopping Online

We've already discussed one of the major benefits of shopping online: convenience. Not having to fight traffic, wade through crowds, and deal with salespeople are all positive benefits—not to mention trying to squeeze comparison-shopping into an already busy life. Who has time these days to visit three to six stores to price a single item?

A second benefit is price. With a little effort, you can usually find what you want for a substantial discount online. However, it's important to find out what the final in-hand price is. The final in-hand price is the amount of money you have to spend to get the product to you. When you make a purchase online, the final in-hand price will include the product's cost minus any discounts or coupons, plus any applicable taxes, packaging or handling fees, and the cost of shipping. Most online stores will allow you to see the final in-hand price before you provide your billing information or at least before you press the final confirm or submit order button. Pay very close attention to the final price, so you can compare true costs from multiple online and brick-and-mortar stores.

By shopping online, you may be able to avoid paying sales tax. If the online store is based outside of your state, you may not have to pay sales tax. This can be a savings of up to 10 percent, depending on the state you live in. As the cost of your item goes up, the dollar amount you can save on sales tax increases as well.

 If you do a lot of online shopping or make high-dollar purchases online, you may want to check with your state revenue agency to see what the guidelines are for your state. In some states you have to pay sales tax if the purchase is over a certain dollar amount.

There's no other way to evaluate the prices from multiple stores as quickly and easily as you can online. Just open multiple Web browsers, surf to different stores, fill your virtual shopping carts, proceed to checkout, and look for the final price. Depending on the item, you might want to compare as few as three stores, or as many as a dozen if the product is fairly expensive.

Online Auctions

Retailers aren't the only people taking advantage of the Internet to sell goods. Many individuals now sell items over the Internet using online auction sites. If you like spending your Saturdays attending estate, farm, or collectible auctions, you're going to love bidding online.

You've probably already heard of eBay, which is the most well-known online auction site, but there are several others, many of them devoted to specific kinds of items. The great thing about online auctions is that they take place all the time (no need to get up early on Saturday mornings to find the best deals), and you can find thousands upon thousands of items upon which to bid.

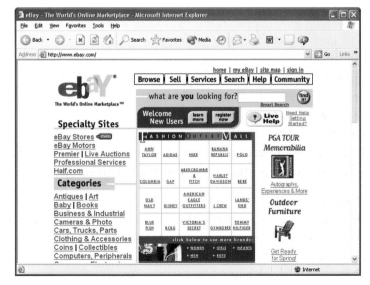

Individuals and companies offer the items you bid on at online auctions. If you're the top bidder when the bidding period expires, you've purchased the product. The bidding period will be clearly posted on the auction site, and you'll be notified via e-mail at the end of the auction if you were the highest bidder.

More About . . . Items at Online Auctions

Just as with auctions you travel to, many of the items offered through online auction are usually used, old, antique, damaged, or repaired. If a used product is just as good to you as a brand-new one, auctions can help you find what you want at a discounted price. If an item you're looking for isn't on the market any longer—say, the manufacturer discontinued the item or it's out of stock—auctions may be your only means to obtain it. However, note that some people do sell unused items that are still in the original packaging on auction sites, so you may be able to find some new items.

When you bid on an item, you're effectively entering into a contract with the seller to purchase the product at your bid price. If you're the highest bidder at the end of the auction, you're obligated to purchase the item. Furthermore, if the highest bidder is somehow disqualified and you're the next-highest bidder, you must purchase the item. The only way to get out of the purchase contract is to retract your bid.

The auction communities at eBay and most other online auction sites have extensive checks to ensure that both the bidder and the seller are protected during a transaction. This means that you will be held responsible for paying for an item in an auction that you win, and at the same time, the seller is held responsible for delivering the product to you as advertised.

Playing Online and Multiplayer Games

One of the most fun interactive activities you can participate in online is to play games with other people, no matter where the players are. You can play backgammon with a complete stranger who lives in Budapest, chess with an old college buddy on the East Coast, and cards with your grandson in Chicago.

An online game is any game you play on the Internet, whether it's a single-player game or involves many people from all over the world. Online games include board games, card games, word games, logic games, traditional-style video games, and fantasy games. Games played between two or more people are called multiplayer games.

 Not all online games require more than one person to play, so if you're more interested in practicing your chess techniques or brushing up on your solitaire skills by yourself, you can do that, too.

MSN Zone Games and Windows XP

Windows XP includes several games that you can play against other opponents over the Internet, including Internet Backgammon, Internet Hearts, Internet Checkers, Internet Reversi, and Internet Spades.

To play one of these five games, establish your Internet connection and then launch the game from the Games section of the start menu (click **start**, **All Programs**, and then **Games**). For example, if you want to play Internet Backgammon, perform the following steps once Windows XP is up and running:

❶ Click **start**, point to **All Programs**, point to **Games**, and then click **Internet Backgammon**. The MSN Zone.com Backgammon welcome screen appears.

❷ Click **Play**.

10

❸ The gaming program connects to the gaming server and finds an opponent for you. Once an opponent is found, the backgammon game board appears and the game can begin. To start the game, click **Roll**.

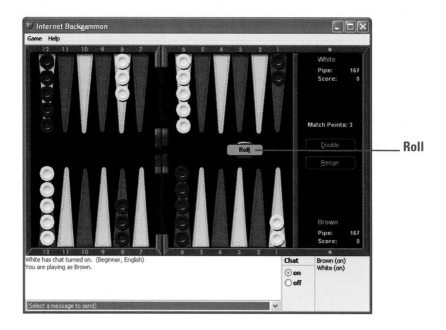

Roll

❹ If you need help learning how to play Backgammon or how to control the interface, click the **Help** menu and then click **Backgammon Help Topics**.

 The five games included with Windows XP are just a sampling of the games offered through the MSN Zone.com online gaming service. You can check out any of the hundreds of online games offered through the MSN Zone by accessing the zone.com URL through your Web browser.

Multiplayer Gaming Sites

If you already own stand-alone computer games such as Microsoft Links or Monopoly Casino (just to name a couple), you can play those games with other players using the games' multiplayer mode. To play computer games in multiplayer mode, the computers either need to be connected to a network or connected, via the Internet, to a multiplayer gaming site.

Every gaming site is different, and the configuration necessary to play a multiplayer game online is also different for each game. Be sure to read the help instructions for your games and the gaming Web site. If you need help, contact the technical support staff for the gaming Web site.

Communicating with E-mail

When you sign up with an ISP or online service, typically at least one e-mail address is included with your account. Using e-mail, you can exchange messages with people next door or across the globe. Although e-mail can't replace "real time" communication (telephone, video conferencing, etc.) or the sound of another person's voice, it does open up many new avenues for interaction.

To send and receive e-mail, you need an e-mail client program on your PC; there are many to choose from. The Windows XP operating system includes a version of Outlook Express. Some alternative e-mail clients are Eudora and Microsoft Outlook (a full-featured version of Outlook Express included with Microsoft Office).

Although many e-mail clients include unique features or extended capabilities designed to entice users, every e-mail client shares a set of common functions. Because we know you already have Outlook Express on your PC, we'll use it as our example and teaching tool for this chapter. After you learn how to use Outlook Express, you can apply that knowledge to any other e-mail client you might run into.

10

The Outlook Express Inbox screen is where most common e-mail activities take place. From here you can:

- ✦ Read e-mail messages
- ✦ Print e-mail messages
- ✦ Delete e-mail messages
- ✦ Compose new e-mail messages
- ✦ Communicate with e-mail servers
- ✦ Reply to messages
- ✦ Forward messages
- ✦ Use your address book

Reading a Message

When you receive an e-mail message, Outlook Express displays information about it—such as the sender, the message subject, and the date and time it was received—in the window's upper-right pane, called the message-list pane.

To get the hang of reading messages using Outlook Express, let's look at the default message Microsoft sends to your Inbox the first time you use the program—the one with the subject "Welcome to Outlook Express 6." Click this message once in the message-list pane, and the message's contents appear in the window's bottom pane. You can use this pane, called the selected message display pane, to quickly preview messages, using the scroll bar on the right side of the pane to view the entire message if you wish. Alternatively, for a better view, you can open the message in a separate window:

❶ Double-click the message in the message-list pane.

❷ A new window opens, displaying the contents of the message. Click the **Maximize** button if the message window is not already maximized.

 Although maximizing the message window helps you read its contents more easily, you may still need to use the scroll bars to see the entire contents of the message.

As shown in Figure 10-4, the message-display window shows four key details about the message in the area above the message body:

- ✦ **From.** This reveals the sender's identity.

- ✦ **Date.** The date listed here reflects the date and time that the sender sent the message to an outgoing e-mail server. This information may differ from what's shown in the main Outlook Express window's message list; the difference in time indicates how long it took the message to travel from the sender to your Inbox.

- ✦ **To.** This denotes the identity of the recipient.

✦ **Subject.** The Subject line provides a way for the sender to identify, categorize, or label an outgoing e-mail message.

The message-display window includes many of the same toolbar buttons as the main Outlook Express program window when the Inbox is selected. These buttons perform the same functions for both windows, but in a message-display window, buttons act only on the open message. In the Outlook Express window, buttons act against the selected message in the message-list pane.

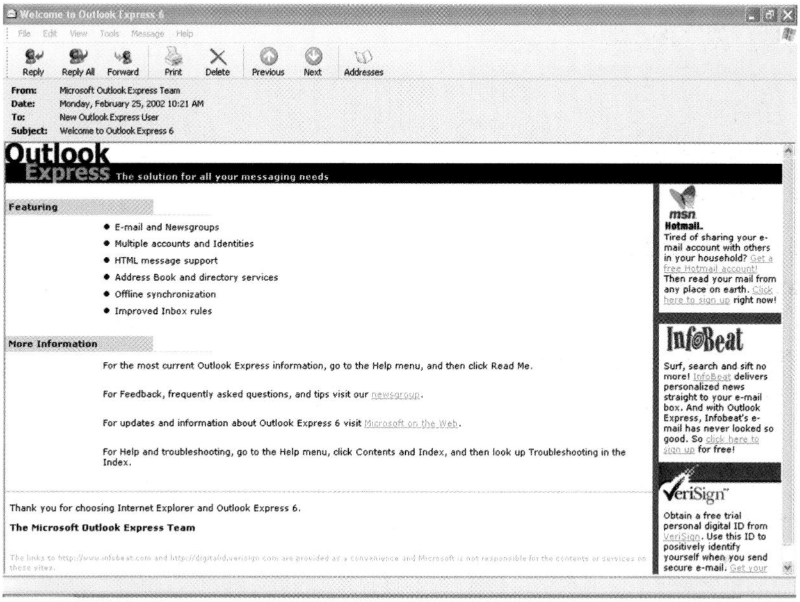

Figure 10-4 An Outlook Express message-display window.

Printing a Message

Printing an e-mail message is as simple as printing any other document. Just select or open the message, and then click the **Print** button. If you want to change default print settings, click the **File** menu then **Print** to open the Print dialog box.

Deleting a Message

After you've read a message, you can decide whether you want to keep it or delete it. To delete a message that is open in its own window, click the **Delete** button in the message-display window's toolbar. Alternatively, you can delete messages from the Outlook Express window. To do so, select the message in the message-list pane that you want to delete, and then click the **Delete** button in the toolbar.

Deleted messages migrate to the Deleted Items folder. By default, this folder retains all deleted items until you empty it; it doesn't automatically empty itself or remove old messages unless you tell it to do so. You can recover deleted messages as long as they remain in the Deleted Items folder.

Composing a New Message

To create and send a message to someone, perform the following steps:

 If this is your first time using e-mail, compose and send a message to yourself by typing your own e-mail address in the **To** field in step 2. That way, you'll have an e-mail message you can use when you learn how to reply to and forward messages in the sections that follow.

1 In the Outlook Express window, click the **Create Mail** button. The New Message window opens.

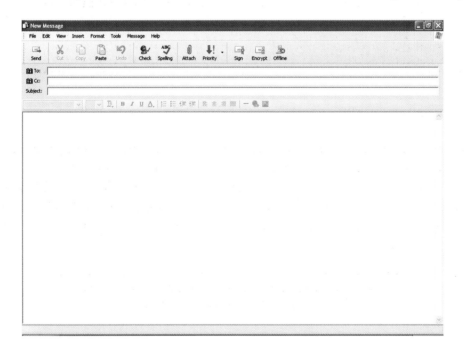

2 In the **To** field, type the recipient's e-mail address. If the message is intended for multiple recipients, type each recipient's e-mail address here, using commas or semi-colons to separate them.

 In the section "Using Your Address Book" later in this chapter, you'll learn how to use your address book to enter the recipient's address in the To field, as well as how to use the Cc field.

3 In the **Subject** field, type a meaningful subject. For example, if you're writing a friend to invite her to dinner, you might type *Dinner* in the Subject field. You could leave the subject blank, but then your recipient wouldn't know what your message was about until they read it.

4 Type a salutation or greeting in the work area, and then type your message and signature.

5 Click the **Send** toolbar button in the New Message window.

If you are connected to the Internet, clicking the Send button sends the message to your outgoing e-mail server. If you are not connected, the message is placed in the Outbox folder. Messages in this folder will be sent to your outgoing e-mail server the next time you connect to that server (discussed in the next section).

More About . . . Composing Messages

Some messages may take longer than others to compose. If you are interrupted halfway through the process of composing a message, you can save it in your Drafts folder until you are ready to work on it again. To do so, click the **File** menu and then click the **Save** command. When you're ready to work on the message again, simply double-click the **Drafts** folder to open it; your message should be displayed in the Draft folder's message list. Double-click the message to open it in its own message-display window. When you finally send the message, it will be removed from the Drafts folder.

Communicating with E-mail Servers

To send or receive e-mail, your e-mail client must communicate with outgoing and incoming e-mail servers. Once you are online and have opened your e-mail client, a simple click of the Send/Receive toolbar button initiates communication. Clicking the Send/Receive button instructs the e-mail client to send all messages in the Outbox to the outgoing-mail server and to download any messages waiting for you on the incoming-mail server into your Inbox.

 You must have an open Internet connection to send or receive e-mail. If your Internet connection is not already established, clicking the **Send/Receive** button may initiate a dial-up connection.

10

To test your configuration and to ensure that the message you created in the previous section is delivered, perform the following steps:

1 Log on to your ISP or online service.

2 In Outlook Express, click the **Send/Receive** toolbar button. Your message should appear in your Inbox.

If you do not see the message you sent to yourself, wait **30 seconds**, and repeat step 2.

When you are online, Outlook Express sends any messages you compose immediately, and checks for new incoming messages every 30 minutes.

The Sent Items folder stores a copy of each message you send. If you ever need to review a message or want to send the same message to someone else, you can find it in the Sent Items folder.

Replying to a Message

If someone sends you a message to which you want to reply, you can easily do so by clicking either the Reply toolbar button (to respond only to the sender) or the Reply All toolbar button (to respond to the sender and any other people who received the original message). Your reply message will include the original message and any additional text you type.

To reply to a message either from the Outlook Express window or the message-display window, perform the following steps:

1 Select or open the message in your Inbox to which you want to reply (in this example, the message you sent to yourself).

② Click either the **Reply** button or the **Reply All** button. A new message window opens; notice that the To line lists all intended recipients, and the original Subject line is prefixed with Re:. Also, the message body includes a copy of the original message.

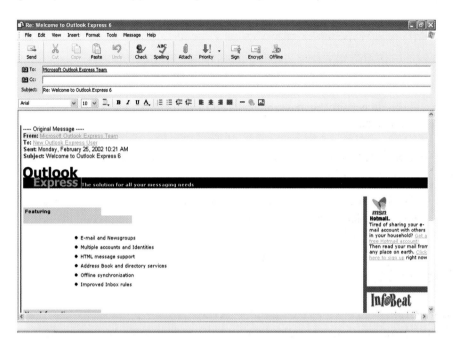

③ The blinking insertion point should already be in the top-left corner of the message area. If not, use your mouse to place it there by clicking, and then type your reply.

④ Click the **Send** toolbar button to send the message or place it in your Outbox.

Forwarding a Message

If you receive an e-mail message containing a good joke, a great recipe, or some other interesting tidbit, you may want to forward it to a friend. When you forward a message, you send it to a new recipient without retyping its contents.

Forward

To forward a message either from the Outlook Express window or the message-display window, perform the following steps:

① Select or open the message in your Inbox to which you want to reply (in this example, the message you sent to yourself).

② Click the **Forward** button. A new message window opens with a blank To line. Notice that the original Subject line is prefixed with Fw:, and that the message body includes a copy of the original message.

10

3 Enter one or more e-mail addresses in the **To** field. For this exercise, type your own e-mail address to forward the message to yourself.

4 Click the **Send** toolbar button to send the message or place it in the Outbox.

Using Your Address Book

You can use your address book as your own personal contact list. Your address book retains all e-mail addresses you add to it, as well as other personal contact information you choose to define.

There are several ways to add contacts to your address book, but one of the easiest is to do the following:

1 In the message-list pane, right-click a message you've received from the person you want to add to your list of contacts. Alternatively, if the message is displayed in its own window, right-click the person's e-mail address in the From field.

2 A shortcut menu appears. Click the **Add to Address Book** command.

Once an e-mail address is in your address book, you can quickly and easily add it to the To line of an outgoing e-mail message. Here's how:

1 Click the **To** button on the message-display window. The Select Recipients dialog box opens.

❷ Click the recipient's name in the left column.

❸ Click the **To** button.

❹ The name now appears in the To field in the Message recipients column. Click **OK**.

Notice in step 3 that there are actually three buttons to choose from:

✦ **To.** Click this button if the person you chose in step 2 is the message's primary recipient.

✦ **Cc.** Click this button if the person you chose in step 2 should also receive the message, but is not a primary recipient. For example, if you are e-mailing a co-worker about a project, you might add your boss's name to the Cc: line of the e-mail message to advise her of the information. ("Cc" stands for "carbon copy.")

✦ **Bcc.** Click this button if you want the person you selected in step 2 to receive the message, but you don't want other recipients to know. ("Bcc" stands for "blind carbon copy.")

To manage the contacts stored in your address book, click the Addresses button in the Outlook Express window, or double-click a contact in the Contacts pane in the lower-left corner of the window.

10

Tips and Troubleshooting

Just like any other piece of equipment, such as your furnace or air conditioner, your PC needs regular, simple maintenance and may sometimes require troubleshooting to work at its best. In this chapter, you'll learn how to determine what version of Windows your PC runs and how to keep your operating system and software programs updated. You'll also discover why you should be vigilant about protecting your PC from virus infection and how to use anti-virus software. Finally, you'll learn how to troubleshoot some common PC problems.

Identifying Your Operating System

Many versions of Windows look similar—so similar, in fact, that it can be hard to tell which version is running on your PC. The design and layout of the desktop, start menu, and taskbar (also known as the graphical user interface, or GUI) for Microsoft Windows 98, Windows 98 SE, Windows Me, and Windows 2000 look more or less alike. Likewise, Windows XP Home and Windows XP Professional appear very similar, differing only in a few features and capabilities.

In previous versions of Windows, the name of the operating system appears on the left side of the start menu. Windows XP, however, does not display its name there. Fortunately, there's a quick and easy way to determine which version of XP is running on your PC. Follow these steps:

1. Click the **start** button, and then click **My Computer**. The My Computer window opens.
2. In the **Help** menu, click **About Windows**. The About Windows dialog box opens.
3. The version appears in a color logo at the top of the About Windows dialog box or is listed in text form. Click **OK** to close the About Windows dialog box.

Updating Your System

Windows XP is designed to be a stable and robust operating system for both home and network users. Even so, software released by even the most cautious manufacturer may contain imperfections (which may include errors, also known as software bugs, or potential security compromises, also known as security holes), which are discovered only after customers put a product to the test. In response, software vendors typically release code corrections known as patches or security fixes to repair such problems.

Microsoft is concerned about keeping your PC as secure and up-to-date as possible, and distributes update files for Windows XP via the Internet. You can configure your PC to download and install such update files for you using Automatic Update, or you can handle them manually by running Windows Update.

Using Automatic Updates

Soon after you install or configure Windows XP, you'll notice an icon in the notification area that looks like a globe bearing the Windows XP logo. Click this icon, called the Dynamic Update icon, to open the Automatic Updates tab in the System Properties dialog box, shown in Figure 11-1.

The Notification Settings area of this tab includes three options:

✦ Download the updates automatically and notify me when they are ready to be installed.

✦ Notify me before downloading any updates and notify me again before installing them on my computer.

✦ Turn off automatic updating. I want to update my computer manually.

11

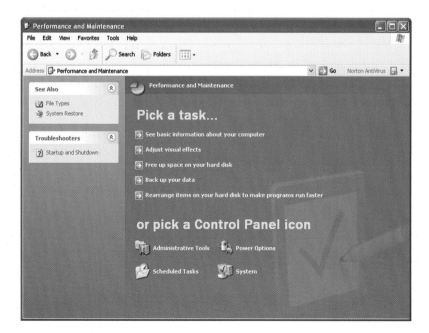

Figure 11-1 The Automatic Updates tab in the System Properties dialog box.

To proceed, make a selection and click **OK**.

To change the settings in the Automatic Updates tab, follow these steps:

1 Click the **start** button, and then click **Control Panel**.

2 The Control Panel window opens displaying the Category view mode by default. Click the **Performance and Maintenance** category.

3 The Performance and Maintenance category window opens. Click the **System** icon.

④ The System Properties dialog box opens. Notice that this screen looks like the Automatic Updates dialog box (see Figure 11-1).

⑤ Select the preferred option, and click **OK** to close the System Properties dialog box.

⑥ Click the **Close** button to close the Performance and Maintenance window.

Scanning Your Machine with Anti-virus Software

Just like you and I, computers are susceptible to viruses. In computer terms, however, a virus is a program that can damage your PC or prevent it from working properly. Viruses can infect program files, document files, image files, music files, system files, and even e-mail messages. Your PC can contract a virus from opening an infected file from a floppy or CD, from opening an attachment in an e-mail message, or even by downloading something from a Web site.

To protect your PC, anti-virus software is recommended. Anti-virus software scans your PC for viruses and removes them before they can do any harm. It can also actively monitor your PC's memory and scan all downloaded files and incoming e-mail messages to stop virus infections before they occur.

Many anti-virus software packages are available, including Symantec's® The Norton AntiVirus®, McAfee's VirusScan®, and Trend Micro's PC-Cillin®, just to name a few. No matter which tool you select, however, keep the following important issues in mind:

✦ Because new viruses appear daily, and because the anti-virus software companies must continually find ways to quarantine viruses, it's important to download and install updates for such virus definitions regularly. Most anti-virus programs do this automatically. If you update manually, downloading updates every two weeks is usually sufficient, except when harmful infections become news.

✦ To avoid infection from downloaded files, e-mail messages, and other incoming data, it's essential that you configure anti-virus software to scan your memory and all incoming data actively. Also, it's a good idea to configure your anti-virus program to scan every file on your PC regularly. In most cases, a once-a-week scan is sufficient.

✦ Whatever anti-virus program you choose must support your operating system; otherwise, that program won't work properly.

Because every anti-virus software tool is different, we can't provide you with a step-by-step guide to installing and using them. Most of these products include a general virus

11

scan capability that you can execute from the main program window, or as a menu selection. Likewise, most products will ask you if they should quarantine or delete any infected items they encounter (quarantine saves the infected file to a special directory on your PC; deleting gets rid of the file completely—the latter is the safest option, when available). Most anti-virus products include excellent instructions, so you should have no problems installing and configuring them on your own. (If you get stuck, don't hesitate to call the vendor's support line or contact the company that sold you your PC.)

Exiting Frozen Programs

Now and then, you may encounter a problem when running various software programs on your PC. For example, a program might freeze or hang—that is, it might stop responding to the mouse or the keyboard, or it might not display properly on the monitor screen. Sometimes, the operating system might present an error message to tell you that something is wrong. When a program freezes, or error messages appear, that failure may stem from a problem with the program itself, a problem with the operating system, or a problem arising from interaction among other active programs. Alternatively, the problem could just be a fluke.

When you encounter such a problem, it may take one or more of the following actions to resolve the issue: wait it out, exit the frozen program, log off, or as a last resort restart your PC.

More About . . . Preventing Problems

Once you get your system up and running again, you might want to look for an update or patch for the program to prevent it from happening again. You can typically find program updates on the Web site of the company that makes the program in question; check the site's Support or Download section for details. If you can't find what you need, call the company's technical support line.

You may also need to update Windows XP to prevent your system from hanging again. Refer to the section "Updating Your System" earlier in this chapter for more information.

Wait It Out

In some cases, your system may appear to be frozen when, in fact, it is simply in the process of performing an intense calculation or some other resource intensive task. If you suspect this is the case, or if you haven't saved your document for a long time and want to avoid losing information it contains, then your best bet is to wait. The system may restore itself after it completes the task. If the system responds within 10 minutes or so, save your document, exit the program, and restart your system. If after 10 minutes the system is still frozen, however, it's unlikely that the program will return to normal. If so, it's best to move on to the next option: exiting the frozen program.

 From this point on, any of the actions you perform as you attempt to unfreeze your system will result in the loss of any information you have not yet saved. Let this be a warning to you: Make a habit of saving your documents regularly to prevent data loss. Saving every five to 10 minutes is a good idea.

Exit the Program

If you've waited for your system to restore itself to no avail, it's best to attempt to exit the frozen program while allowing other programs and the operating system to keep working. There are two ways to accomplish this; be sure to try both before moving on to the next procedure:

✦ Use the taskbar button's shortcut menu

✦ Use the Task Manager

If after you attempt to exit a program, it remains open but is still frozen, it's best to move on to the next option: logging off your system.

Exit Using the Program's Taskbar Button

To exit a frozen program using its taskbar button, perform the following steps:

❶ Right-click the program's button in the taskbar. A shortcut menu appears.

❷ Click the **Close** command.

❸ Wait for the End Program dialog box to open. If it opens, continue to step 4. If the program exits without displaying the End Program dialog box, however, you are finished; you need not perform additional steps.

 If the program fails to close, but the End Program dialog box does not open in two minutes or so, repeat steps 1 through 3 again.

❹ In the End Program dialog box, click **OK**, **Yes**, or **End** to terminate the program.

Exit Using Task Manager

Another way to exit a frozen program while allowing other programs and the operating system to keep working is to use the Task Manager. To launch the Task Manager and access its Applications tab (shown in Figure 11-2), do one of the following:

✦ Press the **CTRL+SHIFT+ESC** key combination.

11

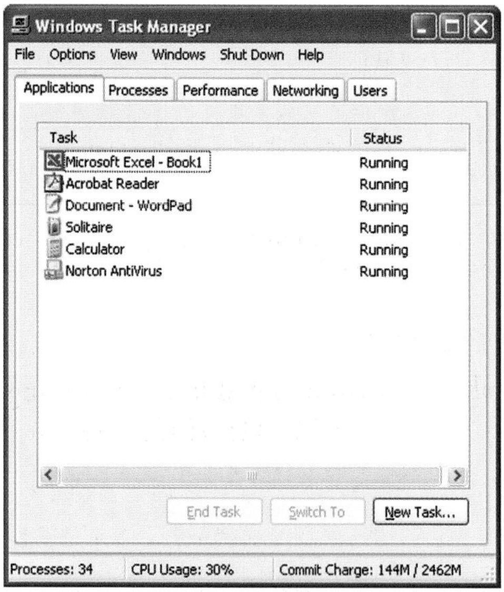

![Windows Task Manager screenshot showing the Applications tab]

Figure 11-2 The Applications tab in Windows Task Manager.

◆ If your Windows XP Professional or Windows XP Home system is a stand-alone system or a member of a workgroup, you can use the **CTRL+ALT+DEL** key combination. However, on other systems, especially network clients, the **CTRL+ALT+DEL** key combination opens the Windows Security dialog box. In the Windows Security dialog box, you can click the **Task Manager** button.

◆ Right-click an empty area of the taskbar, click the **Task Manager** command in the shortcut menu that appears, and then click the **Applications** tab, if necessary.

The Task Manager's Applications tab names every active program. To the right of this list is a column stating the status of each program. If a program is working properly, its status appears as "Running." If a program is frozen, however, its status appears as "Not Responding."

To use the Task Manager to close or terminate a program that is not responding, perform the following steps:

1 In the Task Manager's Applications tab, click the name of the program whose status is listed as "Not Responding."

2 Click the **End Task** button.

3 Wait for the End Program dialog box to open. If it opens, continue to step 4. If the program exits without displaying the End Program dialog box, however, you are finished; you need not perform additional steps.

As in the preceding section, if the program fails to close, but the End Program dialog box doesn't open in two minutes, repeat steps 1 through 3 again.

4 In the End program dialog box, click **OK**, **Yes**, or **End** to terminate the program.

Log Off

If you've attempted to close the frozen program, but your system is still not responding, your best bet is to log off and then log back in. This stops all programs currently running on your desktop.

To accomplish this, do the following:

1. Click the **start** button, and then click **Log Off**.
2. In the Log Off Windows dialog box, click **Log Off**.
3. If an End Program dialog box opens, click **OK**, **Yes**, or **End** to terminate the program. If no such dialog box opens, continue to step 4.

 As noted previously, if a program fails to close, but the End Program dialog box doesn't open in two minutes, repeat steps 1 through 3.

4. When you see the Windows Welcome logon screen, log back on.

If the program remains frozen even after you've taken all steps outlined in the preceding paragraphs, there's only one option left: You must restart your PC. Hopefully, you can force a shutdown and restart. To do so, try the following:

1. Click the **start** button, and then click **Turn Off Computer**.
2. In the Turn off computer dialog box, click the **Restart** button.
3. If an End Program dialog box opens, click **OK**, **Yes**, or **End** to terminate the program. If no such dialog box opens, continue to step 4.
4. After the computer shuts down and restarts, the Windows Welcome logon screen appears. Log back on.

 Again, if the program fails to close, but the End Program dialog box does not appear in two minutes, repeat steps 1 through 3 again.

If this restart process fails, you must resort to powering down your PC manually using its power button, then switch it back on to restart.

Troubleshooting Your PC

Although troubleshooting your PC may seem mysterious now, over time you'll develop the skills you need to diagnose and resolve problems with your computer. As you gain experience using your PC and work through issues as they arise, your ability to troubleshoot will improve. Here are several important tips to help you better troubleshoot your system:

✦ **Stay calm and be patient.** Getting angry or trying to rush won't make troubleshooting any easier. Take your time and keep a clear head.

✦ **Quit all programs and restart your computer.** Quitting all programs and restarting your computer gives it the opportunity to clear and refresh its cluttered memory.

✦ **Check for obvious problems.** Because many problems revolve around loose connections or cables, it's a good idea to check these first. Make sure all cables

11

are securely attached both to your PC and to the connected device, such as your printer, modem, speakers, etc. Make sure the device is turned on before changing any of its settings.

✦ **Check the power supply.** If a device fails to turn on, check their power supplies. If they show a green indicator light (for those that have them), or are slightly warm to the touch (for those that lack indicator lights), chances are good they're working properly. If they're showing red indicators or are room temperature, they probably aren't working properly (and may need to be replaced).

✦ **Focus on software issues.** Most hardware problems are software-related. The device might require an updated driver or some setting modifications in order to work properly.

✦ **Read the screen.** When a problem occurs, a message usually pops up on the screen. Write down the message exactly as it appears, so you can relay the message to a technical support person if necessary.

✦ **Change only one thing at a time.** As you attempt to fix your PC, take things one step at a time, eliminating possible problems with your machine methodically. Make one change to your system, such as updating the driver, changing a single configuration setting, etc. Then test your PC to see if that change helped. If not, reverse or undo that change, then make another change, and test again. Continue making changes one at a time until the problem is resolved. That way, you'll know exactly which change resolved the issue, and you'll be able to fix the problem easily should it occur again in the future.

✦ **Ask yourself the right questions.** When did the problem start? Is the problem always present or only when you enter certain commands? Asking the right questions can help you zero in on the cause of the problem.

✦ **Read the documentation.** An owner's manual is included with most devices and programs; check this manual for a troubleshooting table or list of common questions and issues.

✦ **Make notes.** Take notes on the problems you encounter with your PC and what steps you take to resolve them. Include both successful and failed actions. This information will be useful if a problem ever repeats itself. Additionally, if you ever need to call tech support or take your PC in for repairs, you'll be able to tell them exactly what kinds of problems your PC has had and what you tried to do to fix them.

◆ **Check the manufacturer's Web site.** Most manufacturers have a support area where you can view a FAQ (Frequently Asked Questions) list, search a database for help, and download software updates.

◆ **Never be afraid to ask for help.** If you can't resolve your computer's problem in a reasonable amount of time, call someone, be it your PC manufacturer or reseller, a custom computer shop, or a PC service center. Chances are, they'll be able to help.

The PC Won't Boot

The most frustrating problem you may encounter with your PC is if you can't get it to power on and start. Although there are a few easy ways to resolve this issue in the short term, it can be a sign of bigger problems. To address this problem, perform the following steps. After each step, try to start the PC to see if the problem is resolved.

1 Make sure the PC's power outlet is working. Plug something else into that outlet, such as a lamp, to check.

2 Firmly press the power button on the front of your PC once or twice; be sure you press it all the way in. If that doesn't work, try pressing the button in for 10 seconds or so.

3 Disconnect and reconnect every cable attached to the PC, and then try to turn the power on again.

4 A damaged keyboard or mouse can cause a short circuit that prevents the PC from booting. This is a safety feature to prevent further damage to other PC components. To determine whether this is the case, disconnect the keyboard and mouse and then try powering on your machine.

If these efforts are unsuccessful, consider the following:

◆ If the fan next to the power-cord plug on the back of the system unit case turns on, that indicates your PC's internal power supply is working, but that the PC's motherboard may be damaged or that the on/off switch on the front of the system unit case is not working.

◆ If the fan does not turn on, it could indicate that your PC's internal power supply has failed. In some cases, a power supply that doesn't power on simply indicates a blown fuse or breaker. (The fuse or breaker prevents electrical surges from reaching the delicate internal components of the PC.) In many cases, that fuse or breaker can be reset. In some instances, however, once the fuse or breaker is tripped, the power supply must be replaced.

◆ If the on/off switch on the front of the system unit case doesn't click or work, it is broken and must be replaced.

◆ If the power indicator(s) lights up on the front of the case but nothing else happens, the hard drive(s) or the motherboard could be damaged.

If the PC powers up but still doesn't boot, it could require a system restoration. This can be accomplished by using the system restoration CDs that ship with your Gateway PC or by calling upon the services of a professional computer technician.

Utilizing Online and Professional Help

If you encounter a problem that is not addressed by this chapter, you can take advantage of the troubleshooting tools provided by your manufacturer. Most manufacturers have a support area on their Web site where you can view a FAQ (Frequently Asked Questions) list, search a database for help, and download software updates.

Windows XP includes a Help and Support Center that you can access by clicking **start** and then selecting **Help and Support** (see Figure 11-3). Help and Support contains a variety of topics and information to help you get more out of your PC and help guide you through any technical issues you might encounter.

Figure 11-3 Use the Windows XP Help and Support Center to troubleshoot many problems.

Professional help is aid from any computer technician. That technician can be from your point of purchase, the manufacturer of your PC, individual hardware device or specific software, a custom local repair shop, or a dedicated technical support service. Be sure to have your sales paperwork handy (this includes the receipt and any technical description of the PC or peripheral device). You can refer to this paperwork to look up make and model information or verify warranty coverage. If you need a technician to service your PC, be sure to give them a copy of that paperwork. This saves time and effort answering many questions they might otherwise need to ask you.

You'll usually find technical support contact information either on the company's Web site or in the user manual that accompanied their product. If you are unable to locate proper technical support access information, contact your point-of-sale and inquire how to obtain technical support. As a last resort, you can find local computer repair and technical support centers listed in the phone book under "Computers."

Glossary

.NET Pronounced dot-Net, an operating system design intended to erase the boundaries between personal computers and the Internet.

activation A security measure enacted by Microsoft to guard against software piracy. When Windows XP asks you to activate your copy, you must do so within 30 days by phone or on the Internet, or the software stops working.

active program The program whose window has a dark title bar; title bars for inactive program windows are subdued in color. In addition, an active program's taskbar button appears depressed, while taskbar buttons of inactive programs do not.

address book A feature in an e-mail client program that allows you to store e-mail addresses and other personal contact information.

address field In a Web browser, shows a URL for the Web site currently on display in the workspace area of the application window.

AGP (Accelerated Graphics Port) A type of motherboard connection used to connect to high-speed video cards. Most motherboards have only one AGP port.

anti-virus software A special type of program that scans your PC for viruses and removes them before they can do any harm. It can also actively monitor PC memory and scan all downloaded files and incoming e-mail messages to stop infections before they occur.

attachment Any type of file, such as a document, picture, music, archive, or another e-mail message, that you send over the Internet along with your e-mail message.

autorun A program that automatically opens a file or begins an installation routine when a CD is placed in a computer's CD-ROM drive.

booting The sequence of steps that activates a PC. The start-up process includes powering up, testing hardware, launching the operating system, and establishing an account in which to operate. Generally called starting.

browse (your computer) To look through a display or listing in search of something of interest, perhaps a specific document or program.

burner A device that records data to recordable CD and DVD discs.

burning a CD The process of writing data to a CD-R or CD-RW.

buttons Common dialog controls; you click buttons to execute commands or to apply whatever settings you've selected in a dialog box. Common buttons include Close, Cancel, Apply, Print, Open, and Save; usually, the name on a button defines its function.

cable modem Typically an external device that uses a NIC (network interface card) to connect a computer to a cable service that offers Internet access.

cc (carbon copy) An e-mail feature that allows you to send a copy of your message to people other than the primary recipient.

CD (compact disc) A medium-capacity optical storage medium; CDs are like DVDs, but store only 650 and 700 MB of data, which may be audio or video, but is likely to be software or other data.

CD-R (compact disc-recordable) A CD storage medium that can be recorded only once, but can be played or read many times.

CD-ROM (compact disc-read only memory) A CD storage medium that uses the same type of discs you play in your audio CD player to store computer programs and files; you can read from CD-ROM discs but you cannot write to them.

CD-ROM drive A device that reads CDs. CD-ROM is a read-only medium; the "ROM" in its name stands for Read-Only Memory.

CD-RW (compact disc-rewritable) A CD storage medium on which data can be stored and then erased as needed; thus, CD-RW discs are reusable.

central processing unit (CPU) *See* CPU.

check boxes Controls, found in a dialog box, used in lists of options when more than one option can be selected, or when a single option can be turned on or off.

click The most common mouse action; to click, position the pointer over an object on your screen. Then press and release the primary mouse button.

closed The final stage of recording data to a disc (CD or DVD), which makes a recordable disc readable on an ordinary CD or DVD drive.

communication devices Various types of hardware that allow two or more PCs to communicate. Such devices normally connect to expansion cards inside the system unit, or to external serial, USB, FireWire, PC Card, or NIC connections.

computer administrator user account A privileged Windows XP account that can create, manage, and delete user accounts; change PC and user configurations; install programs; and access all files on a PC.

connections The cables, plugs, connectors, and ports needed to add devices to your system unit.

Control Panel A Windows icon that provides access to all the utilities needed to configure your PC and install new hardware reside within the Control Panel.

CPU (central processing unit) The "brain" of a computer. Its role is to interpret and carry out instructions, perform computations, and control devices connected to the PC. A dual processor PC has two CPUs, for more computing power.

critical updates Patches for your Windows-based PC that fix or prevent potentially serious problems, such as security holes or bugs.

desktop The main work area or computing environment in the Windows environment that appears once you start up and log on to your PC.

details pane The right side of the window in My Computer or Windows Explorer that displays the contents of a folder or drive.

device driver *See* driver.

dialog box Used by Windows XP to solicit user input, they often appear as a result of selecting certain menu commands or performing other actions.

double-click An action performed with the primary mouse button to initiate some activity; similar to clicking, except you click twice, quickly, without moving the mouse.

dragging A technique that enables you to move text, graphics, files, and objects of any kind on your screen. Simply position your mouse pointer on the object to be moved, press and hold down the primary mouse button, and slide the mouse. Also called clicking and dragging.

driver A special type of software that allows a specific hardware device to communicate with a PC. Without a driver, hardware devices won't work. Sometimes called a device driver.

DSL (digital subscriber line) modem A digital telephone service used to provide high-speed Internet access. It requires specific hardware.

DVD (digital versatile disc) A high-capacity optical storage medium, a DVD looks the same as a CD, but can store between 4.7 and 17 GB of data which may be audio, video (it's a preferred format for movies), or other information.

DVD-R (digital versatile disc-recordable) A DVD storage medium that can be written to only once. DVD recorders and discs use much narrower tracks than those used on CDs, allowing them to store up to seven times more data than CDs.

DVD-RAM (digital versatile disc-random access memory) A storage technology for computers that uses a type of disc similar to those used in a TV's DVD player. DVD-RAM discs can be read and written many times, so they may be used like a computer's hard disk drive.

e-mail Any of a number of messaging systems used on the Internet. E-mail may be plain text, but messages can include pictures, formatting, and animation. You can also attach just about any kind of file to an e-mail message.

e-mail account A service you get from an ISP, online service, or an independent Internet company such as Yahoo or Hotmail.

e-mail address Represents the person and their location to which to send e-mail on the Internet, similar to how the address of your home allows people and companies to send mail to you. An e-mail address includes a user name separated from an ISP, online service, or company name by an @ sign.

e-mail client A program used to read and send e-mail messages.

e-mail message Written communication, similar to a letter, that is sent from one computer to another. Also called electronic mail.

FAQ (Frequently Asked Questions) A list of common questions with their answers, normally compiled by technical support operations to provide ready access to information and answers in high demand (or of high interest).

file A container for text, programs, documents, images and other stored items on a PC; also, objects in a PC file system where actual documents and data reside.

file name extension Groups of three or more characters that appear to the right of the rightmost period in a file name; Windows uses this data to associate programs with files.

Files and Settings Transfer Wizard A Windows wizard you can use to move your personal data files and desktop settings from one PC to another.

floppy drive A storage device that reads and writes to 3.5" diskettes (also known as floppy disks), a common removable storage medium. Typical floppy disks hold up to 1.44 MB.

folder A named container in a PC file system that contains other objects (either files or other folders, called subfolders); used to organize files and containers into a recognizable and navigable folder structure.

freeze What programs are said to do when they stop responding to the mouse, keyboard, or fail to display properly on the monitor screen. Sometimes the operating system might present an error message to tell you that something is wrong.

graphical user interface (GUI) The use of graphics, windows, and icons instead of text to interact with PC users.

guest account A pre-defined Windows user account that allows anyone to log on and use the computer without entering a password.

hard drive A storage device typically located inside the system unit. A hard drive stores both the instructions a computer needs to run and any data a user types in and saves.

hardware All physical objects or devices attached to a PC, including the monitor, keyboard, mouse, printer, and the system unit itself qualify as hardware.

Help and Support A Windows icon that provides access to a Help and Support Center; the first, best place to go when you need help with Windows XP.

home page A predefined Web site that your Web browser loads each time it opens.

hyperlinks Text or graphical elements on a Web page that you click to jump to another Web page. Hyperlinks usually appear underlined, in a different color than surrounding text. Also called links.

icon A small graphic with a text label; it represents an object or a shortcut to an object stored in another location.

IEEE 1394 (FireWire) A high-speed peripheral interface that is much faster than USB 1.1 and supports as many as 127 devices (the same as USB). PCs with built-in FireWire support usually have two such ports: one in the back and one in the front.

inbox The area in which new messages sent to your e-mail address appear when they're downloaded to your computer.

inkjet printer A printer that produces output by spraying microscopic drops of ink onto the paper as it passes through the printer. Most inkjet printers can print both color and black images.

input hardware Any device used to enter information (text, sound, or images) into a PC. Examples of input hardware include keyboards, mice, scanners, digital cameras, and microphones. Also known as input devices.

insertion point A blinking vertical bar that appears in the upper-left corner of a program's workspace to indicate where text will appear when you start typing.

Internet A physical network of millions of computers around the world. This network allows the computers to communicate back and forth. Also called the information superhighway.

Internet Explorer A Web browser you can use to surf Web sites located on the Internet throughout the world.

ISP (Internet service provider) A company that provides Internet access to subscribers.

keyboard A PC input device, used to enter numbers, letters, symbols, and even control commands in your PC, typically connected to a PC through a PS/2 or USB connection.

LAN (local area network) A group of connected computers typically located in a single room or building, connected to a single hub.

laser printer A printer that produces output by using lasers to adhere and bond a powdered toner onto paper. Laser printers produce detailed high-quality images.

limited user account An unprivileged Windows XP account for regular users that can only create or delete its own password, change its own picture, theme, and desktop settings, access files it creates, and access files in the Shared Documents folder.

local printer A printer that is connected to a computer is local to that computer.

log off In the Windows environment, to close your desktop and return to the logon screen. This gives the next user quick access to the logon screen.

log on In the Windows environment, to select a user account and provide a password, if one is required, to gain access to the PC.

Maximize button The middle button in the group of three Windows controls at the top right of every window. It looks like a single Window icon and causes the window to fill the entire display when clicked.

media Individual items, such as floppy disks, CDRs, CD-RWs, DVD-Rs, tapes, or Zip/Jaz cartridges, that you can insert into or remove from a removable storage device.

menu bar A list of words or names, called menu names, which appears just below the title bar and just above the first toolbar in a window.

message body The actual information contained in an e mail.

message header A brief description of the contents or purpose of the message and the e-mail addresses of all recipients.

Minimize button The minus-sign-shaped button leftmost in the group of three Windows controls at the top right of every window. Use this button to hide its program window, thus freeing up space on your desktop, without shutting down the program.

modem A device that allows a PC to communicate with other PCs using a standard phone line. A modem can be an expansion card installed inside the system unit or an external device connected via a USB or serial cable.

monitor A device that displays visual output for a PC. A tube monitor looks like a television set—heavy, large, and boxy. A flat-panel monitor is narrow in profile and provides crisp, clean images that are more vibrant and brilliant than some tube monitors.

motherboard The foundation of a modern PC; it provides numerous sockets or ports to accommodate and interact with other devices, such as CPU, memory and expansion cards, with cables to link to hard drives and CD-ROM/DVD drives. Any motherboard accepts only specific CPU and memory types. Also called a mainboard.

mouse A small device that you use to move the mouse pointer on a PC screen; designed to help control graphical user interfaces of all kinds; connects to a PC using serial, PS/2, or USB connections.

mouse pointer A small, white, left-pointing arrow that appears somewhere on your screen that the mouse can direct to select objects, buttons, menus, or other screen items.

MP3 player A portable device that plays back digitally recorded music. MP3 players have either a large amount of memory or a hard drive on which digital music is stored.

MSN Explorer A version of Internet Explorer specifically configured for the MSN Internet access service.

My Computer A Windows icon that opens a window showing all hard drives, folder shares, and removable storage devices available on your PC.

My Network Places A Windows icon that becomes useful when your PC is connected to a network. Its window displays all shared data accessible from the network, with links to common tasks and other network locations.

network Two or more computers connected so they can share resources and exchange data.

network interface card (NIC) A special type of PC adapter that connects the PC to some type of network medium and facilitates network communications.

network printer A printer that is accessible by a network user, even though the printer is not attached directly to his or her computer.

notebook computer A fully functional computer that's about the size of a college textbook (or even smaller) with a built-in screen, keyboard, and pointing device. Also called a laptop.

notification area That portion of the far-right end of the taskbar, where small icons from certain applications show you they're running but don't appear on the desktop.

object A named Windows element, which may be a file, folder, printer, or some other kind of Windows resource, that uses a unique "address" to identify it among all other resources on your PC.

object path The location information that identifies any object's exact location on a Windows PC as a prefix to the object's name. *See also* path.

object-selection field An area that lists one or more options. In most cases, you can select only a single item at a time; the selected item is highlighted.

online game Any game you play on the Internet, whether it's a single-player game or involves many people from all over the world.

online service A company that provides Internet access to members or subscribers.

operating system (OS) The fundamental software that runs on a PC (or other computer) to create a working computing environment that supports access to the hardware and permits other programs (word processing, Web browser, e-mail client, and so forth) to run.

option buttons Windows controls used to select only one item from a list of options. To select an option button, click it; when selected, a dot appears inside the button.

Outlook Express A Microsoft e-mail program that enables you to read and send e-mail to anyone with an address on the Internet

output hardware Any device that produces information from a PC system. Examples of output hardware include the monitor, printers, loudspeakers, and those storage devices that can create or update files, media, and much more. Also known as output device(s).

pane A subsection of an application window, a dialog box, or a subsection of the workspace within an application window that is usually outlined and named.

parallel port Normally used to attach printers to a PC, the parallel port on a system unit is always female. Usually, only a single external device can connect to a parallel port.

passport An electronic identification badge that provides access to sites and services on the Internet through a single log on or account.

patches Program or Windows updates that include bug fixes (corrections provided to repair known problems), security updates (to prevent unauthorized access to your data), or database updates (to give a program the latest data it needs to perform its job).

path A roadmap to a particular resource or object, such as a file, folder, or printer. A path to a network printer, for example, consists of the name of the computer to which the printer is connected followed by the name of the printer itself.

PC card A common connection type used mainly on notebooks, where PC card devices plug into PC card slots.

PCI (Peripheral Component Interconnect) The most widely used type of connection points on a motherboard. Some PCs have only two PCI slots; others have as many as six.

peripherals Hardware devices that connect to a PC. Some peripherals are required, such as a monitor; others are optional, such as a scanner. Also known as add-on devices or external devices.

personal computer (PC) A device that processes information. A PC can deliver education and entertainment, manage personal information and records, and support essential business activities. You can also use a PC to type letters, send messages, interact with others, listen to music, play games, learn new skills, and more.

personal data assistant (PDA) A portable computer designed to act as an organizer, note taker, communication device, and so forth. PDAs are fast, functional, and include various user-friendly applications to help you organize business and personal activities.

pointer images Specific shapes such as I-beams, pointing fingers, and so forth that Windows uses to indicate the current function or status of the mouse pointer.

printer A device that prints text or graphical images from a computer. A printer can produce black or color output on paper and typically connects to a PC using a parallel or USB port.

program A piece of software designed to work with your PC's operating system to perform one or more tasks and to manage various types of information (such as text, numbers, and images). Also called an application.

PS/2 A common type of serial port on PCs. Two female PS/2 ports occur on most desktop PCs: one for the mouse, the other for the keyboard. Most notebooks have only a single PS/2 port, which can be used to attach either an external mouse or keyboard.

random access memory (RAM) Temporarily stores data, software, and the operating system while a PC is operating; everything in RAM is temporary.

Recycle Bin A temporary storage location for recently deleted files; use it like a wastebasket.

removable storage Any storage device that uses readable and writable media that can be removed from the drive. They include floppy drives, CD and DVD drives, tape drives, and Zip/Jaz drives.

restore point A method of capturing a snapshot of Windows desktop settings and preferences to which you can return in the future.

right-click Click the secondary button once over an object to cause a related shortcut menu to appear.

screen saver A utility available in many operating systems that displays a picture on the screen after a specified period of inactivity has lapsed to prevent an unchanged image from being burned onto your monitor screen. You have a wide range of images to choose from and can include your own preferred picture.

scroll bars Special window positioning controls that appear when a window isn't big enough to display the entire contents of a document or page. These allow you to scroll up and down or left and right through the page or document so you can view all its contents.

Search A Windows icon that provides access to a Search tool; use this tool to locate files and folders on your local system or the network. You can also use this tool to search for pictures, music, video, documents, computers, and network users.

search engine An Internet program that performs its search against Internet content. It uses automated software tools known as spiders, robots, or crawlers to create and maintain a database of information about the Internet. The spiders, robots, or crawlers download nontrivial content from every single Web page they can find on the Internet.

shared network resources Anything on a network that is accessible by users, such as drives (files and folders), printers, and scanners.

shortcut An object that enables you to associate an icon on the desktop or in some other convenient location with a specific resource.

shortcut menu A menu that is context- or content-sensitive; here, the object or objects under the mouse pointer determine what commands appear in such a menu.

Shutdown A process whereby Windows XP saves important data still resident in memory, closes the desktop and the operating system, and then powers off the PC.

software All programs, tools, or utilities that permit PCs to perform all kinds of tasks, and handle data and services for users. Software is intangible, but still quite real.

software bugs Imperfections sometimes found in software released by even the most cautious manufacturer.

speakers Devices that produce audio output from a PC. Through speakers or a set of headphones, you can hear operating-system sounds, music, sound effects, and so forth.

SSL (Secure Sockets Layer) Used to encode and protect personal information sent between your Web browser and another computer.

start button The colorful start icon at the left side of the taskbar, where you access all Windows programs and commands as well as any installed programs.

start menu To launch this menu, click the start button on the task bar. From here, you can start programs, find documents, configure your computer, and more.

status bar An area located along a window's bottom edge that displays program-specific information and messages.

subfolder Folders that reside inside other folders, designed to help you locate documents, programs, and data more easily.

submenu If a submenu is present, an arrow appears beside a command in a menu. Select and execute submenu commands just as you do commands on main menus.

surfing the Web Entering URLs and clicking hyperlinks to explore various Web sites on the Internet.

surge protector A power-outlet multiplier and an electric-spike protector; includes a fuse or built-in circuit breaker that disconnects power if a spike occurs.

system unit A box or enclosure that contains many smaller electronic components, such as a motherboard, processor, memory cards, video card, one or more hard drives, floppy drive, CD-ROM drive, and power supply. A system unit may be called a case or a tower.

taskbar The long bar at the bottom of your Windows screen, this visual element reports on open applications, provides access to the start menu, and includes a notification area.

text box A text field in a dialog box in which you can enter data using your keyboard.

theme A set of appearance options that work as a named group and that create a quick and easy way for you to personalize Windows XP.

third-party program Any program that is not included with the operating system. This includes programs from Microsoft as well as any other software company.

throughput A rating of how much data can be sent or received by a device within a specific amount of time; normally measured in Kbps, Mbps, or Gbps.

Tiles The default view for files and folders in My Computer and Windows Explorer (a bright yellow file folder and a picture of a hard disk) is called Tiles. There are four other views.

title bar A Windows element (at the top of the window frame) that displays the name of the program or function underway. When a window contains an open document, the title bar also displays that document's file name.

toolbar The icons that appear below the menu bar but above the workspace. Click buttons on a toolbar to access common functions or perform common tasks.

uninterruptible power supply (UPS) A battery and power conditioner; connects between the wall outlet and your PC. If power fails, a UPS can supply a PC with power from its battery, where uptime depends on battery size how much power attached devices draw.

URL (Universal Resource Locator) A special kind of Internet address that you must supply to access a Web site.

USB (Universal Serial Bus) A newer, faster type of peripheral port on PCs that supports up to 127 devices per port. USB is available in two versions: 1.1 and 2.0. The 2.0 version offers throughput speeds greater than FireWire.

user accounts A means that Windows XP uses to identify individual collections of personal data. Each person who uses a PC should have his or her own user account.

user profile In Windows operating systems, this refers to the collection of settings that defines how your desktop looks, sounds, and operates. As you use your PC and change its look and feel, your user profile becomes unique.

views Ways to view information displayed in My Computer and Windows Explorer. Click the Views button (far right of the button bar) to see all five views.

Web browser A software utility used to access the World Wide Web.

Web page A document formatted for viewing over the Internet through a Web browser A Web page often includes links to other Web pages or Web sites.

Web server A computer on the Internet that houses one or more Web sites; Web browsers communicate with Web servers to access Web pages.

Web site A collection of online documents maintained by a group or an individual that addresses one or more topics.

Web-based e-mail E-mail accessed from a Web site instead of from software installed on your computer.

window A rectangular area displayed on your desktop that contains numerous common elements, such as a workspace, toolbars, a menu bar, and other standard controls. Almost every Windows-based program uses a window as its primary interface.

window corner Either the bottom left or right corner of a program window, this control enables you to alter the height and width of a window at the same time.

Windows Media Player A utility that can play back many types of music and video files, Internet radio, Internet TV, and CDs.

wizard A window similar to a dialog box, in that it presents a series of options from which you must choose. Unlike a dialog box, which presents all available controls, options, and selections, a wizard presents controls one at a time, in a specific order.

workspace The area in a window between the toolbars and the status bar. In some programs, the workspace acts like a piece of paper in the real world, and uses the keyboard to enter input; in others, it acts more like an interface. You interact with it by clicking buttons, choosing options from drop-down lists, and so on.

World Wide Web A vast collection of interconnected graphical or textual information available to those with Web browsers and network (or Internet) access. Often called the Web.

Index

print/printing
   button, 100, *221,* 222, 233
   dialog box, *105, 108,* 233
product keys, 49
program interface window, 94–103
programs, 121–31, 245–49. *See also*
   software
PS/2 ports, 25, 27, *46,* 258

R

random access memory (RAM),
   12–13, 14, 258
Recycle Bin, 61, 190–91, 258
Refresh, 34, *221,* 222
removable storage, 13, 259
restart, 63, *65*
Restore Defaults button, 166
restore down button, 96–97
restore point, 259
right-clicking, 68, 69, 70–71,
   77–78, 83, 259

S

satellite connections, 37
Save As dialog box, *106,* 117–20,
   156–57, 165
Save as type list, *117,* 119, 165
Save button, 100, 119–20, *157,*
   180
Save in list, *117,* 119, *157*
saving files, 109, 116–20, 156–57
scanners, 32
screen saver, 259
scroll bars, 100, 105–6, 259
scrolling, 68, 79, 82, 105
Search, 168, 195–97, 259
secondary mouse button. *See* right-
   clicking
security, online, 224–26
selecting objects, 72–73, 76–78,
   113, 115, 127
serial ports, 25, 26, 37
shared network resources, 259
shopping, 35, 223–28
shortcut menus, 77–78, 118,
   130–31, 150, 157–58
shortcuts, *80,* 81, 96, 122, 127–28,
   259
shortcuts, creating, 178–81
shutdown, 62–65, 259
sizing handles, 102–3
software. *See also* files
   anti-virus, 245–46, 254
   drivers, 9, 55, 255
   e-mail client, 220, 255
   frozen programs, 246–49

installing, 211–13
overview, 8, 9, 90–93, 258, 259
product keys, 49
shortcuts to, 178–79
third-party, 91, 260
unfreezing, 246–48
updating, 243–45
working with, 94–103, 121–31
software bugs, 243, 259
software programs. *See* programs
Solitaire, 85–87, *91*
speakers, 36, *44,* 47, 48, 49, 259
SSL (Secure Sockets Layer), 259
Standby button, 63
standby mode, 63, 64, *65*
start button, 53, 54, 61, 259
start menu, 53, 74, 92, 259
static guards, 41
status bar, *94,* 100–101, 259
Stop button, *221,* 222
storage devices, 13–17, 116–17,
   118
subfolders, 155, 259
submenus, 99, 259
surfing the Web, 220–23, 259
surge protectors, 40, *45, 46,* 47,
   259
SVGA/VGA ports, 25, 27
switching accounts, 146–49
Switch User button, 148
system files, 76
system unit, 259
system unit case, 10, *44*

T

taskbars, 61, *96,* 122, 123–26, 247,
   259
Task Manager, 64, 247–48
text, 110–16, 113, 115, 158, 260
theme, 260
throughput, 38, 260
Thumbnails view, 169
Tiles view, 169, 260
Tile Windows, 127–30
time zone, 50
title bars, *94,* 95, 260
toolbars, *94,* 99–101, *221,* 233,
   260
Tools menu, 166
ToolTips, 62, 73, 100, 124, 155
touchpads, 83–84
trackballs, 83–84
troubleshooting
   booting, 48, 163, 251–52
   frozen programs, 246–49
   slow system speed, 97
   tips, 249–51

turning off your PC, 62–65

U

Undo, 114, 130, 131
uninterruptible power supply
   (UPS), 40–41, 260
Up One Level button, *117,* 118
URL (Uniform Resource Locator),
   219, 260
USB ports, 25, 28, 260
user accounts
   adding, 135–36, 145–46
   logging off, switching, 146–49
   .NET passports, 142–45
   overview, 134, 137–42, 139–41,
     260
User Accounts window, 135–41
user names, 50
user profiles, 260

V

VGA ports, 25, 27, *46*
video cards, 23, 24
View menu, 98–99, *117,* 118
Views button, 169, 260

W

Web, 216–20, 260. *See also* e-mail;
   Internet
Web browsers, 217–18, 220–23,
   259, 260
Web servers, 142, 194, 220, 260
wheel (mouse), 68, 79
window corners, *94,* 102–3, 260
windows
   displaying multiple, 122–26,
     127–31
   moving, 95, 98
   overview, 127–31, 260
   program interface, 94–103
Windows Explorer, 101
Windows Media Player, *90,* 204–8,
   260
Windows Movie Maker, *91*
Windows Welcome screen, 148–49,
   249
Windows XP, 49–55, 90–91,
   242–43
wireless devices, 30, 31
wizards, 108–9, 260. *See also specific*
   wizards
WordPad, *91,* 92–93
wordwrap, 115–16
workspace, *94,* 96, 101, 181, 260
World Wide Web, 216–20, 260. *See*
   also Internet

GATEWAY, INC. END-USER LICENSE AGREEMENT

IMPORTANT - READ CAREFULLY: This End-User License Agreement (EULA) is a legal agreement between you (either an individual or an entity), the End-User, and Gateway, Inc. ("Gateway") governing your use of any non-Microsoft software you acquired from Gateway collectively, the "SOFTWARE PRODUCT".

The SOFTWARE PRODUCT includes computer software, the associated media, any printed materials, and any "online" or electronic documentation. By turning on the system, opening the shrinkwrapped packaging, copying or otherwise using the SOFTWARE PRODUCT, you agree to be bound by the terms of this EULA. If you do not agree to the terms of this EULA, Gateway is unwilling to license the SOFTWARE PRODUCT to you. In such event, you may not use or copy the SOFTWARE PRODUCT, and you should promptly contact Gateway for instructions on returning it.

SOFTWARE PRODUCT LICENSE

The SOFTWARE PRODUCT is protected by copyright laws and international copyright treaties, as well as other intellectual property laws and treaties. The SOFTWARE PRODUCT is licensed, not sold.

1. **GRANT OF LICENSE.** This EULA grants you the following rights:
   - **Software.** If not already pre-installed, you may install and use one copy of the SOFTWARE PRODUCT on one Gateway COMPUTER, ("COMPUTER").
   - **Storage/Network Use.** You may also store or install a copy of the computer software portion of the SOFTWARE PRODUCT on the COMPUTER to allow your other computers to use the SOFTWARE PRODUCT over an internal network, and distribute the SOFTWARE PRODUCT to your other computers over an internal network. However, you must acquire and dedicate a license for the SOFTWARE PRODUCT for each computer on which the SOFTWARE PRODUCT is used or to which it is distributed. A license for the SOFTWARE PRODUCT may not be shared or used concurrently on different computers.
   - **Back-up Copy.** If Gateway has not included a back-up copy of the SOFTWARE PRODUCT with the COMPUTER, you may make a single back-up copy of the SOFTWARE PRODUCT. You may use the back-up copy solely for archival purposes.

2. **DESCRIPTION OF OTHER RIGHTS AND LIMITATIONS.**
   - **Limitations on Reverse Engineering, Decompilation and Disassembly.** You may not reverse engineer, decompile, or disassemble the SOFTWARE PRODUCT, except and only to the extent that such activity is expressly permitted by applicable law notwithstanding this limitation.
   - **Separation of Components.** The SOFTWARE PRODUCT is licensed as a single product. Its component parts and any upgrades may not be separated for use on more than one computer.
   - **Single COMPUTER.** The SOFTWARE PRODUCT is licensed with the COMPUTER as a single integrated product. The SOFTWARE PRODUCT may only be used with the COMPUTER.
   - **Rental.** You may not rent or lease the SOFTWARE PRODUCT.
   - **Software Transfer.** You may permanently transfer all of your rights under this EULA only as part of a sale or transfer of the COMPUTER, provided you retain no copies, you transfer all of the SOFTWARE PRODUCT (including all component parts, the media and printed materials, any upgrades, this EULA, and the Certificate(s) of Authenticity), if applicable, and the recipient agrees to the terms of this EULA. If the SOFTWARE PRODUCT is an upgrade, any transfer must include all prior versions of the SOFTWARE PRODUCT.
   - **Termination.** Without prejudice to any other rights, Gateway may terminate this EULA if you fail to comply with the terms and conditions of this EULA. In such event, you must destroy all copies of the SOFTWARE PRODUCT and all of its component parts.
   - **Language Version Selection.** Gateway may have elected to provide you with a selection of language versions for one or more of the Gateway software products licensed under this EULA. If the SOFTWARE PRODUCT is included in more than one language version, you are licensed to use only one of the language versions provided. As part of the setup process for the SOFTWARE PRODUCT you will be given a one-time option to select a language version. Upon selection, the language version selected by you will be set up on the COMPUTER, and the language version(s) not selected by you will be automatically and permanently deleted from the hard disk of the COMPUTER.

3. **COPYRIGHT.** All title and copyrights in and to the SOFTWARE PRODUCT (including but not limited to any images, photographs, animations, video, audio, music, text and "applets," incorporated into the SOFTWARE PRODUCT), the accompanying printed materials, and any copies of the SOFTWARE PRODUCT, are owned by Gateway or its licensors or suppliers. You may not copy the printed materials accompanying the SOFTWARE PRODUCT. All rights not specifically granted under this EULA are reserved by Gateway and its licensors or suppliers.

4. **DUAL-MEDIA SOFTWARE.** You may receive the SOFTWARE PRODUCT in more than one medium. Regardless of the type or size of medium you receive, you may use only one medium that is appropriate for the COMPUTER. You may not use or install the other medium on another COMPUTER. You may not loan, rent, lease, or otherwise transfer the other medium to another user, except as part of the permanent transfer (as provided above) of the SOFTWARE PRODUCT.

5. **PRODUCT SUPPORT.** Refer to the particular product's documentation for product support. Should you have any questions concerning this EULA, or if you desire to contact Gateway for any other reason, please refer to the address provided in the documentation for the COMPUTER.

6. **U.S. GOVERNMENT RESTRICTED RIGHTS.** The SOFTWARE PRODUCT and any accompanying documentation are and shall be deemed to be "commercial computer software" and "commercial computer software documentation," respectively, as defined in DFAR 252.227-7013 and as described in FAR 12.212. Any use, modification, reproduction, release, performance, display or disclosure of the SOFTWARE PRODUCT and any accompanying documentation by the United States Government shall be governed solely by the terms of this Agreement and shall be prohibited except to the extent expressly permitted by the terms of this Agreement.

7. **LIMITED WARRANTY.** Gateway warrants that the media on which the SOFTWARE PRODUCT is distributed is free from defects in materials and workmanship for a period of ninety (90) days from your receipt thereof. Your exclusive remedy in the event of any breach of the foregoing warranty shall be, at Gateway's sole option, either (a) a refund of the amount you paid for the SOFTWARE PRODUCT or (b) repair or replacement of such media, provided that you return the defective media to Gateway within ninety (90) days of your receipt thereof. The foregoing warranty shall be void if any defect in the media is a result of accident, abuse or misapplication. Any replacement media will be warranted as set forth above for the remainder of the original warranty period or thirty (30) days from your receipt of such replacement media, whichever is longer. EXCEPT AS EXPRESSLY SET FORTH HEREIN, GATEWAY, ITS SUPPLIERS OR LICENSORS HEREBY DISCLAIMS ALL WARRANTIES, EXPRESS, IMPLIED AND STATUTORY, IN CONNECTION WITH THE SOFTWARE PRODUCT AND ANY ACCOMPANYING DOCUMENTATION, INCLUDING WITHOUT LIMITATION THE IMPLIED WARRANTIES OF MERCHANTABILITY, NON-INFRINGEMENT OF THIRD-PARTY RIGHTS, AND FITNESS FOR A PARTICULAR PURPOSE.

8. **LIMITATION OF LIABILITY.** IN NO EVENT WILL GATEWAY, ITS SUPPLIERS OR LICENSORS, BE LIABLE FOR ANY INDIRECT, SPECIAL, INCIDENTAL, COVER OR CONSEQUENTIAL DAMAGES ARISING OUT OF THE USE OF OR INABILITY TO USE THE SOFTWARE PRODUCT, USER DOCUMENTATION OR RELATED TECHNICAL SUPPORT, INCLUDING WITHOUT LIMITATION, DAMAGES OR COSTS RELATING TO THE LOSS OF PROFITS, BUSINESS, GOODWILL, DATA OR COMPUTER PROGRAMS, EVEN IF ADVISED OF THE POSSIBILITY OF SUCH DAMAGES. IN NO EVENT WILL GATEWAY, ITS SUPPLIERS' OR LICENSORS' LIABILITY EXCEED THE AMOUNT PAID BY YOU FOR THE SOFTWARE PRODUCT. BECAUSE SOME JURISDICTIONS DO NOT ALLOW THE EXCLUSION OR LIMITATION OF LIABILITY FOR CONSEQUENTIAL OR INCIDENTAL DAMAGES, THE ABOVE LIMITATION MAY NOT APPLY TO YOU.

9. **Miscellaneous.** This Agreement is governed by the laws of the United States and the State of South Dakota, without reference to conflicts of law principles. The application of the United Nations Convention on Contracts for the International Sale of Goods is expressly excluded. This Agreement sets forth all rights for the user of the SOFTWARE PRODUCT and is the entire agreement between the parties. This Agreement supersedes any other communications with respect to the SOFTWARE PRODUCT and any associated documentation. This Agreement may not be modified except by a written addendum issued by a duly authorized representative of Gateway. No provision hereof shall be deemed waived unless such waiver shall be in writing and signed by Gateway or a duly authorized representative of Gateway. If any provision of this Agreement is held invalid, the remainder of this Agreement shall continue in full force and effect. The parties confirm that it is their wish that this Agreement has been written in the English language only.

"Rev.3 9/24/98".